THE WORLD IN THE TWENTIETH CENTURY

LOUIS L. SNYDER
Professor of History
The City College of New York

THE ANVIL SERIES
under the general editorship of
LOUIS L. SNYDER

ROBERT E. KRIEGER PUBLISHING COMPANY
HUNTINGTON, NEW YORK

To

DEAN AND MRS. MORTON GOTTSCHALL

Original Edition 1955
Reprint Edition 1979

Printed and Published by
ROBERT E. KRIEGER PUBLISHING COMPANY, INC.
645 NEW YORK AVENUE
HUNTINGTON, NEW YORK 11743

Copyright © 1955, 1964 by
Louis L. Snyder
Reprinted by Arrangement with
D. VAN NOSTRAND COMPANY, INC.

Printed in the United States of America

Library of Congress Cataloging in Publication Data

Snyder, Louis Leo, 1907-
   The world in the twentieth century.

   Reprint of the revised edition published by D. Van Nostrand, Princeton, N.J., which was issued as no. 4 in the series. An Anvil original.
   Bibliography: p.
   Includes index.
   SUMMARY: Records the major events in the world from 1900 to the present and includes 25 condensed versions of the key clauses of documents that have exerted the most influence on contemporary developments.
   1. History, Modern—20th century.   I. Title.
[D421.S59 1979]   909.82   79-10024
ISBN 0-88275-909-4

National Series Data Program
ISSN #0570-1062

PREFACE

The history of past centuries has solidified into conventional patterns, which are readily recognizable by most students. On the other hand, the student of twentieth-century history finds himself under a heavy handicap. The chapters of history which he studies are not closed; they are still fluid, unverified, lacking in perspective. He must regard his analysis of trends as temporary and he must postpone his verdicts. He is faced with a tremendous amount of details. His textbooks, rapidly approaching the one-thousand page variety, are becoming as heavy and unwieldy as the Sunday edition of *The New York Times*.

It is the purpose of this volume to boil down the most important historical occurrences since the beginning of the century to fundamentals for an understanding of the period. The unessential is eliminated. An attempt has been made to record all the major significant events and to give the chief actors their historic rôles. The emphasis is upon global proportions. No claim for finality of judgment is made, for the emphasis on patterns is certain to change with the course of the years.

Part I treats the narrative of the twentieth century with provisional interpretation reduced to a minimum. In accordance with the general policy of the Anvil series, Part II is devoted to rigidly condensed versions of the key clauses of those documents that now appear to have exerted the most significant effect on contemporary developments. The Appendix lists instances in which proposals before the United Nations Security Council were vetoed.

I wish to express warm thanks to my colleague, Wallace Sokolsky, for his assistance in reading the proofs.

LOUIS L. SNYDER

TABLE OF CONTENTS

— 1 —

CHARACTERISTICS OF
THE TWENTIETH CENTURY

The World in 1900. Concurrent with the acceler-
ated tempo of the New Industrial Revolution and the
New Imperialism in the closing decade of the nineteenth
century there was an epidemic of minor imperialistic wars
in Africa and Asia. Hitherto, the international struggle for
supremacy had been an exclusively European phenomenon, but now the United States and Japan had the status
of global powers.

The world entered the twentieth century fearful and
divided against itself. The most critical unsolved problem
of the time was the constant threat of war. There was
little sense of moral power among the nations, nor was
there any international organization capable of settling
the recurrent disputes between nations. The cumulative
achievements of science had brought swift changes in
living but also terrible and more destructive weapons.
There was vigor in perfecting the techniques of science,
but it was a vitality of fever, not health. There was as yet
no adequate answer to the crucial question of how to
bring these techniques under control. Men had learned to
control everything except the savageries of human nature
and the confusions of human government. Instead, the
nations of the world competed with one another to make
applied science serve as an instrument of national policy.

Added to the threat of war were such unsolved issues
as the problems of class conflict, poverty, and social
justice. The wealth of the world had increased immeasurably, but there remained a large gap between production
and distribution of this wealth. In addition to the possi-

9

bility of international conflicts there was a danger of class warfare within the industrialized nations.

These were the twin challenges of the new century—how to resolve burning animosities on both the international and domestic scenes. The world of 1900, seemingly progressive and rich in accomplishment, was on the verge of a series of gigantic struggles. "Everybody's nerves are tense," said Colonel E. M. House, special advisor to President Wilson, in the spring of 1914. "It only needs a spark to set the whole thing off." Speaking on the class issue, J. B. Bury, the British historian, uttered a solemn warning in 1913: "If a revolutionary movement prevailed, led by men inspired by faith in formulas (like the men of the French Revolution) and resolved to impose their creed, experience shows that coercion would almost inevitably be resorted to." Both predictions were accurate.

The Historical Pattern. The twentieth century has been variously called the Age of Technology, the Age of Nationalism, the Age of Democracy versus Dictatorship, the Age of World Wars, the Age of the Common Man, and the Age of Freud. Each of these terms describes one strand in a historical pattern. Economically, the century saw an intensification of the Industrial Revolution and extraordinary new developments in communication, transportation, trade, and industry. Politically, the period was distinguished by the intensification of nationalism and by a bitter struggle between democracy and dictatorship. Militarily, the century saw two gigantic World Wars, whose casualties were considerably greater than the 18,-000,000 from the end of the eleventh to the twentieth century. Socially, the nineteenth century was preëminently the Age of the Bourgeoisie; the twentieth saw an advance in the status of the proletariat. Psychologically, the twentieth century under the impulse of Sigmund Freud marked the beginnings of a scientific investigation of the human psyche, human behavior, and the psychopathology of everyday life. The history of the twentieth century is, in reality, a combination of all these developments.

Several monistic interpretations of history, by their very nature, fit the twentieth century into their particular pattern of causation and motivation. Marxists see the twentieth century as fulfilling Karl Marx's prediction of the inevitability of socialism. Arnold J. Toynbee regards it as another phase of his theory of challenge-and-response. Others, notably Pareto, Bergson, and Croce, discuss the century in terms of the rise, maturity, and decay of cultures that have no redeeming faith. Oswald Spengler in his *Decline of the West* saw the present age as one of disillusionment about the past and as one of despair for the future. We are on the downward curve, he insisted, of another historical cycle such as that which involved the ruin of the ancient Roman Empire and its civilization; cosmos turns to chaos and civilization reverts to barbarism. These monistic views are condemned by the pluralistic school of historical causation on the ground that there are several acceptable concepts of history rather than a single correct one.

Specialists in the history of the twentieth century place emphasis upon different basic developments. J. Salwyn Schapiro sees the twentieth century as not just another century, but a new era in civilization, like its predecessors, the thirteenth and eighteenth centuries. He feels that more than any previous period the twentieth century is a century of "one world," created by the almost miraculous advance of science and its offspring technology. Hans Kohn finds the central development to be a dichotomy between the spirit of the West (tolerance, compromise, self-criticism, fair-minded objectivity, reasonableness, and individualism) and the spirit of the East (authoritarianism, the cult of force, the dethronement of reason, fanatical faith in the State, infallible leaders, ruthlessness, barbarism, and slavery). This concept is stated also by Sir Harold Butler, who regards the current cold war not as just a conflict between communism and democracy, but as a struggle between the free ideals of Western civilization and the authoritarian ideas of the East—a struggle between peace and power.

To Hajo Holborn the collapse of the traditional European system is an irrevocable fact of the twentieth century. What is commonly called the "historic" Europe, he says, is dead and beyond resurrection. Carlton J. H. Hayes sees the world of the twentieth century becoming more unified and contracted in some respects, more fragmentary and complex in others. He warns of the central historical (and physical) fact that change always appears much greater at close range than from a distance. "In all probability, the present age of world war, dictatorship, and chaotic art and science will seem to later generations progressively less revolutionary than it appears to us."

New World Situation. The decisive changes of the twentieth century were: the decline of Western European civilization, the deterioration of the British Empire, the new order in Asia, and the rise of the United States and the Soviet Union as leading world powers.

Weakened by wars and revolutions and enclosed between the Atlantic and the natural frontiers of Soviet Russia, Europe lost her traditional dominance. In the words of a European historian, Edmond Vermeil: "Uncertain of herself after a shattering war; with little support from an Africa seething with revolt; squeezed between America and Russia, . . . —a divided and balkanized Europe has to struggle to defend herself . . . , but without being able to choose or create a new order strong enough to maintain the balance between the great forces engaged in conflict." Western Europe may recover and resume its position as the generator of world civilization, but at the present moment this seems to be a remote possibility.

The United States emerged in the twentieth century as the most wealthy and powerful nation on earth. After contributing to the final victory in 1918, the nation was unsuccessful in the vital task of rebuilding a world grievously damaged by four years of war. She had given tremendous material and military aid to her Allies in Europe, but now she withheld the moral support so desperately needed. Rejecting the Wilsonian gospel of a world order, she took refuge in protective isolation. Four years of incredible prosperity before the presidency of Herbert Hoover were followed by the cataclysmic economic crisis of 1929, which spread throughout the entire world. The nation recovered under Roosevelt's New Deal, but, in the meantime, an unrepentent Germany was given a second, this time unhoped-for chance to drive for world power. Overcoming another wave of isolation, the American people supported Roosevelt in his resistance to Hitler. Once again, just when she felt herself to be on the verge of victory, Germany, after advancing deep into the Soviet Union, crashed in ruins. After 1945 the phenomenally prosperous United States assumed the mantle of world leadership once held by Great Britain.

The challenge to American leadership came from the Soviet Union. After the Revolution of 1917, the Bolsheviks liquidated all internal opposition and survived foreign intervention. The new political structure of the Soviet Union was rigidly oriented around despotism, mass discipline, fanaticism, terror, and propaganda, all distinguished by a bitter, implacable hatred of the capitalist world. Leninist-Stalinist ideology erased the slate of the past and introduced a new idea of man and society, denouncing the cultural humanism of the West as an outmoded expression of a decadent bourgeois world. Once the Revolution was solidified, world-revolutionary communism was fused with Russian messianic nationalism, and Bolshevik totalitarianism sought to convert the entire world—a concept for which Trotsky had been rewarded with an assassin's axe. Russian expansionism was something more than the old Pan-Slavism in a new dress. Stepping into the power vacuum after World War II, the Kremlin spread its tentacles in all directions as the drive for power took on global dimensions. European states were engulfed in a new system of satellites. Soviet ideological influence extended to Iran, Afghanistan, China, the Netherlands East Indies, and Indonesia.

Age of Technology. It has been said that all events in history are part of a chain of being in human development and that in every era are to be found the residues of the past and the germs of the future. The twentieth century had its roots deep in the nineteenth. The New Industrial Revolution of the late nineteenth century opened tremendous resources of power, expanded production, and enhanced the wealth of the world. The new century saw an almost miraculous advance of science and technology. Time and space were annihilated by new inventions. For the first time in the history of civilization all parts of the world came into communication with one another. Vast stretches of the earth were telescoped into neighborhoods, and no nation could remain untouched by events on other continents. It seemed that the *humanitas* of the Hellenistic philosophers and the "humanity" of the eighteenth-century rationalists were at last to be realized by the inventions of modern science.

New forms of power appeared in the Age of Technology. A century of steam had been followed by what seemed to be at first a century of petroleum, but within a short period after 1900 it became evident that the new era was to be an age of electricity. Cheap electric power unlocked the energy of coal and utilized water to drive an amazing variety of machines. New sources of power stimulated the development of the factory-plant system and the mass production of goods. As man became more and more dependent upon his machines, he had to find the raw materials required by them. If he could not find them at home, he had to look abroad. Those nations geared to an agrarian economy were at a disadvantage in this race for natural resources. World equilibrium was unbalanced as dynamic, industrialized states began to compete with one another to satisfy their technological appetites. The appearance of new industrial giants— America, Germany, and Japan—was a threat to the prosperity of the old, industrialized nations.

The New Capitalism. The twentieth century saw significant changes in the capitalistic system of production, distribution, and exchange. The new technology called for industrial reorganization in the more advanced nations, particularly in Western Europe and the United States. Giant national corporations were transformed into international cartels. Industrial plants were run by a new managerial class. Concurrent with these changes came the rise of large craft and industrial unions. No longer able to stand aside, governments now became supervisors and regulators of economic activities. The older form of liberal capitalism changed to economic planning. Governments, holding strategic positions in economic affairs, stepped in to guide taxing and spending, contracted or expanded bank credit, controlled the issuing of securities, set maximum and minimum production schedules, and took measures to conserve natural resources. Where the old capitalism functioned for private interest, the new economic planning was conceived to be in the public's interest.

Twilight of Imperialism. Nineteenth-century imperialism continued on at the opening of the twentieth century. The insatiable demand of the machine for raw materials made it imperative for the industrial nations of the earth to obtain ready access to the sources for materials. The older imperialism of Great Britain and France came into head-on conflict with the new imperialism of Germany, Italy, and Japan. These latter "have-not" nations were not impressed with the argument that the backward areas of the earth had already been appropriated; they intended to create new colonial empires even at the risk of conflict. The bitterness engendered by these colonial ambitions was one of the primary causes for the World Wars of the twentieth century.

As the century wore on, imperialism went into retreat, and the old, overflowing vitality of the nations of Europe, which had once planted their flags of empire on every continent, began to disappear. Four old empires died after World War I—the Russian, German, Ottoman, and Austro-Hungarian. The urgent drive to be free stirred among a billion black and yellow men. The remaining empires were rocked by World War II. The Japanese and Italian empires were liquidated, and Germany's second drive for world power was shattered in the ruins of Berlin. The Netherlands relinquished their hold on the once prosperous Dutch East Indies. France, driven from Lebanon and Syria, was on the way out in Indo-China. In the last decade more than half a billion Arabs and Asians have won independence and have established the new sovereign states of India, Pakistan, Indonesia, South Korea, Burma, Ceylon, Israel, Libya, Jordan, and the Philippines. The United States has offered independence to Puerto Rico, and Hawaii and Alaska are close to statehood.

There remain six old empires, governing 172 million people and one-seventh of the world's land surface. Great Britain, learning from defeat, transformed her restless empire into a friendly commonwealth, ruling through freedom instead of force. The British still control thirty-five colonies in five continents; they have poured millions into African development, despite trouble in such white-settled colonies as Kenya. The French Union, still one of the world's greatest empires, was shaken by rebellion in French North Africa and Indo-China. In contrast to British relaxation, French colonial policy remains mercantilist in character, with the colonies supplying France with raw materials, markets, and military manpower, and few concessions made to local autonomy. The Belgian Congo, eighty times the size of the motherland, is still ruled by a tough Belgian administration, which grants no political rights to the natives. The three smaller empires, those of The Netherlands, Spain, and Portugal, manage to hold on in an era of toppling empires. The West has freed some 500 million natives at a time when the new Communist imperialism has enslaved 800 millions.

Political Heritage. The twentieth century inherited from the nineteenth the concept of democracy, with its accent upon human rights and fundamental freedoms, as well as constitutional and representative government. In Western Europe, particularly in Britain and France, and in North America, the functioning of democracy was marked by extension of the franchise and the supremacy of representative institutions. Imperial Russia, however, continued to be an absolute monarchy based on divine right run by an inefficient and corrupt bureaucracy. Bismarckian Germany, despite its liberal constitution in form, was in fact a semi-autocracy. Democracy was virtually unknown in Asia, Africa, and Latin-America. Nationalism, in the nineteenth century almost inseparable from democracy, gradually lost its liberal character and became more and more integral in nature as dissatisfied nationalities sought to implement their national yearnings. The great problem of national self-determination remained unsolved, especially in Europe, where subject peoples demanded freedom from the Russian, Hapsburg, and Ottoman empires. Stirrings of nationalist movements began in India, China, Egypt, and Africa as the century began. A remarkable nationalistic transformation had already taken place in Japan where a backward, feudal people became a sovereign, national state on the Western model within two decades after 1868. National minorities all over the world demanded resurrection in the political age of nationalism.

International Anarchy. From the nineteenth cen-

tury the twentieth inherited a system of international relations based on balance of power. The nations of the
world were divided into three ranks—the great powers,
the middle-sized powers, and the small powers. If any
attempt were made to disturb this balance, the other nations would combine in coalition to prevent aggrandizement. This system was successful in preventing a great
world war from 1815 to 1914, but it was not strong
enough to resist a multitude of civil and national wars.
Burning international animosities were churned up for a
hundred years before 1914. There was no effective international organization outside of the weak Hague Court of
Arbitration founded in 1899. The world atmosphere was
embittered and international confidence was undermined
by rapidly expanding competition in the construction of
military forces. Militarism thrived in an atmosphere of
sword rattling as all the major nations entered the armament competition. French nationalists sought *revanche*
for 1871; Russian nationalists, disgusted with a series of
diplomatic defeats, attempted to restore their prestige by
supporting Pan-Slavism in the Balkans; German nationalists demanded a place in the sun and embittered the
British by insisting upon the construction of a great Navy;
and British nationalists supported the *status quo* in the
face of growing threats from abroad.

Social Impact of Industrialism. The new industrialism stimulated the growth of population, the concentration of people in urban areas, the rise of problems concerned with the metropolis, the decline of illiteracy, and
the appearance of the mass circulation press. The old
class conflict between nobility and bourgeoisie that had
taken place in the early nineteenth century was now succeeded by a struggle between the middle class and the
proletariat. Once the workers became enfranchised and
literate, they formed political parties to further their interests. Socialism became a militant workers' movement
aiming to use political power to advance economic interests. The Socialist movement, worldwide in its scope, was
strongest in those areas where a rigid class system, the
heritage of feudalism, was maintained. Trade unions
emerged as instruments of collective strength to bargain
for the interests of the working class. The pattern of the

social fabric of the world, reflecting the heritage of the past and the economic status of individual classes, began to change in the era of rising industrialism.

Religion. The idea of religious freedom fashioned in the nineteenth century continued on in the twentieth. The American system of separation of church and state was extended elsewhere, but there remained large areas of the world in which religious toleration was not practiced. The Orthodox religion in Russia took a dim view of dissenters, and Jews were savagely persecuted. Non-Catholics were subjected to rigid restrictions in Spain, Portugal, and the Latin-American countries. Mutual hostility among Hindus and Muslims existed in India.

Intellectual Patterns. The breath-taking progress in technical discoveries and the cumulative achievements of science brought about a profound revolution in the thought of man. The intellectual life of the twentieth century was saturated with the new technology. Like the *philosophes* of the Age of Reason, the man of the early twentieth century was an optimist who was certain that civilization was progressing to a higher and higher plane. The next generation would certainly be wiser and better than this one. Many believed that in time liberal ideas would encompass the whole world; they regarded progress as inevitable as the growth of a tree. Herbert Spencer had already proclaimed the new age: "Progress is not an accident but a necessity. What we call evil and immorality must disappear. It is certain that man must become perfect." Men of good will saw a new world in process of formation. The fact that there had been no general war for a century was regarded as indicative of a great future for mankind. Others were less optimistic, warning that new systems of coercion would negate the gains of democratic self-government, national self-determination, religious toleration, and freedom of thought. The explosive Marxian doctrines, emphasizing historical materialism and the inevitability of socialism, provided a new force that was to challenge the optimism of those who foresaw a peaceful world.

Psychological Implications. A well-rounded picture of historical development must include something more than a study of man's economic needs. Modern man attained his intellectual maturity through attempts to think for himself. The magnificent achievements of the Enlightenment were due directly to man's faith in himself and in his own reason. Out of this grew freedom of thought, recognition of the right to disagree, and the rational settlement of arguments and disputes by discussion and compromise.

Gradually over the course of the nineteenth century there arose a growing distrust in reason. Romanticism, at first a protest against rationalism, merged with nationalism. Instead of praising reason and the intellect, the romantic nationalists turned to the heart, the soul, and the blood for inspiration. They glorified the past as a necessary step in national expression. They were convinced that reason was powerless against such biological forces as instincts. The best chance for survival, they said, existed in the warmth and friendliness of the homogeneous group in the nation. Stimulated by this type of thinking, masses of men turned to leaders, witch doctors, and demagogues who urged them to "think with the blood" or adopt a perverted "science of history." Human beings accepted the ideas of worshipping the hero and the cult of force. On occasion, they became victims to new forces far more uncompromising in their opposition to democracy than had ever been the absolute monarchs of the past.

The twentieth century witnessed a high-water mark in this dethronement of reason and the appeal to myths. This development can be understood better by applying the tools of psychological diagnosis, in terms of moral and intellectual decay. A new scholarly trend may be noted in the emergence of a multidisciplinary approach to the study of history, by which historians, social psychologists, anthropologists, and sociologists work together to clarify such historical phenomena as national character.

THE AGE OF NATIONALISM

The Prime Force. Nationalism has been for the last hundred years the prime force of European history. In the twentieth century it became the major force of world history. "Political nationalism," said Sir Norman Angell, "has become for the European of our age, the most important thing in the world, more important than civilization, humanity, decency, kindness, pity; more important than life itself." The chief actors on the stage of present history are nations; their drives, emotions, and interests have been vital in the development of contemporary history. Errors in judgment about the nature of nationalism were responsible in part for the two World Wars of the twentieth century and the subsequent peace treaties.

Like all historical movements, nationalism is deeply rooted in the past. The product of political, economic, social, intellectual, and psychological factors, it emerged over the course of centuries gradually taking on common characteristics. Its first great manifestation was the French Revolution which stimulated and spread the force already in motion. Its composite pattern utilized some of the oldest and primitive feelings of man, including love of birthplace and distrust of the alien. Its character varied from benign love of country to destructive hatred for the foreigner. Although remarkable changes have made one world technologically possible, they have not yet altered drastically the sentiment we call nationalism.

Problem of Meaning. The deceptively simple term nationalism is used to describe what is, in reality, a complex historical phenomenon. Several generations of scholars have devoted their efforts to the task of clarifying the meaning of nationalism. Despite their labors, they have not been able to achieve a unanimity of definition. The fault lies partly in the fact that the

20

meaning of nationalism changes with the course of history. Another difficulty is that nationalism may mean different things to different people. On occasion, different parties within one country utilize the word to express totally divergent views. Much of the confusion may be attributed to nationalists who have a vested interest in maintaining a vagueness of language as a cloak for their aims.

Meaning of Nation. The serious study of the meaning of nationalism and its implications has only recently begun. Many disciplines have contributed to this investigation. Let us examine briefly the work that has been done in several disciplines to clarifying the problem of meaning by directing our attention to three terms— nation, nationality, and nationalism.

The consensus among all scholarly disciplines is that the term nation is tantalizingly ambiguous. The preponderant point of view holds that a nation is not a race, nor is it a state. Language, religion, and territory are important factors in the nation, but none of them is the exclusive determinant of the nation. Geographers point to the basic significance of natural center and environment. Historians regard the nation as the population of a sovereign political state, living within a definite territory, and possessing a common stock of thoughts and feelings that are acquired and transmitted during the course of a common history by a common will. Political scientists see the nation as the formal organization of one people and as an organic unity, the result of organic growth. Sociologists regard the nation as one of the largest and most important collectivities in human society but prefer to use such terms as group, in-group, and social unit instead of the more controversial "nation." Psychologists base the existence of the nation primarily on the behavior of its individuals and seek its meaning in terms of psychological characteristics. Consciousness and emotion, they say, form the cement that binds the nation. Psychiatrists see the nation as made and maintained by an emotionally sustained education in nationhood, beginning with the crucial factor of family life and extended later to the large collectivity. Psychoanalysts look upon the nation as the largest of the social aggregates to which the individual attaches his loyalty, and as the external representation of the super-ego (the inner, unconscious censor).

Meaning of Nationality. A term of the utmost complexity, nationality defies exact definition. It may be used in a concrete (objective, or external) sense (national language, territory, state, civilization, and history), or in an abstract (subjective, internal, or ideal) sense (national consciousness, or sentiment). Nationality does not depend on race, nor exclusively on language. Nationality and state are not synonymous terms. Nationality is not a "folk-spirit," nor is it an emanation of the "World Spirit." The commonly accepted idea that nationality and citizenship are one and the same thing is erroneous.

Historians see nationality as a concept of recent origin, stemming out of the French Revolution, but undergoing a preliminary evolution from instinct to idea, to abstract principle, to dogma. In its concrete sense it may be either political, cultural, or a combination of both. Political scientists place emphasis on the exclusive and separatist character of nationality; it is not entirely political, they admit, but has psychological implications. Sociologists regard nationality as primarily a social category, and in defining it they give weight to such terms as people, collectivity, social unit, and group. Seeing it as a combination of external and internal facts, they admit the impossibility of developing an objective theory of nationality without the assistance of the historian and the psychologist. To psychologists, nationality is a subjective and psychological condition of mind, a spiritual possession, a way of thinking, feeling, and living.

Perhaps the most satisfactory simple definition of nationality is that projected by Frederick Hertz, the British sociologist, who calls it "a community formed by the will to be a nation." This definition combines the main interests of several disciplines—the community (sociology and anthropology), the will (psychology, psychiatry, and psychoanalysis), and a nation (history and political science).

Meaning of Nationalism. The addition of the suffix "-ism" endowed the nation with new excessive traits that made it more than a mere political or cultural community.

A superimposed, artificial sentiment became the final cause of the community. Although deeply interested in the concrete values of nationalism, historians readily admit that, in its ideal sense, it is a psychological fact. Sociologists feel that the key factor in nationalism is the group from which the individual imbibes traditions, interests, and ideals. Anthropologists see nationalism as either a vestige of instinctual behavior or a persistent mode of behavior of the human mind. Psychologists look upon nationalism as a form of the psychologically recognized phenomenon of individuals identifying themselves with symbols that stand for the mass. From the psychiatric point of view, nationalism is a defense mechanism working on a large, in-group scale, by which the group seeks to assure security in a hostile world. It may appear on a rationalistic level, but it is subject, like the individual, to deviant behavior. Three elements of neurosis may be found in nationalism: anxiety, sense of inferiority, and instability. Psychoanalysts direct attention to the psychical processes of nationalism. It offers a response to the individual's need for security and protection. It may be in part a carry-over of parent and family fixation; it may express deep-seated fear and hostility; it may be an outlet for aggression, anxiety, or a sense of inferiority.

The following definition of nationalism, based on a consensus of the various disciplines, is, perhaps, the least objectionable: nationalism, a product of political, economic, social, and intellectual factors at a certain stage in history, is a condition of mind, feeling, or sentiment of a group of people living in a well-defined geographical area, speaking a common language, possessing a literature in which the aspirations of the nation have been expressed, attached to common traditions and common customs, venerating its own heroes, and, in some cases, having a common religion. It should be added that there are exceptions, more or less pertinent, to nearly all the terms used in this definition. Nationalism should be considered first and foremost, a state of mind, an act of consciousness, a psychological fact. It is that socially approved symbol used by modern society in its search for security.

Course of Nationalism.   A century ago it was widely

believed that peace on earth could be assured if only each nation would become independent and united. The idea of individual liberty was transferred to the organic collectivity known as the nation, and it was widely believed that national self-determination was the answer to the problem of differences between countries. The eighteenth century Enlightenment preached the natural goodness of man; the nineteenth century substituted for this belief the idea that collectivities of peoples, or nations, would act as good and peaceful forces as soon as they were able to break away from multi-national states. National independence was the magic key which would result in peace on earth and good-will to men.

The twentieth century saw the shattering of this optimistic faith. The open society appearing in the Western democracies placed a premium upon freedom of the individual—life, liberty, and the pursuit of happiness. But in the twentieth century nationalism spread to Central and Eastern Europe, to countries whose traditions had been authoritarian and which looked with disdain upon the Western concept of individual liberty. This new form of nationalism was adapted to a closed society, in which the place of the individual was considered to be subservient to the authority of the national whole. This new idea of nationalism infected Asia and the Middle East.

This central thesis of the conflict between the open and closed society has been developed by Hans Kohn: "In the last half century many new nation-states were created and many people were 'liberated.' Often these peoples had rightful complaints about inequality of their status and about curtailment of personal liberty. But before the First World War the evolution all over the earth went, recognizing and following the example set by Britain, in the direction of greater equality of status and of growing recognition of individual rights. The creation of the new nation-states after the world wars has in no way strengthened this trend. In many cases it reversed it. Nationalities which had demanded independence from oppression, became oppressors themselves as soon as they were 'liberated.' Innumerable disputes about 'historical' and 'natural' frontiers arose. Long established ties of economic and cultural intercourse were disrupted. The ensuing feeling of insecurity led in many instances to a curtailment of individual liberty, to an increase in armaments, and to a heightening of international tensions. Though national independence brought a great emotional elation to many peoples at the time of its achievement, the historian will ask himself whether this momentary elation is not too dearly bought. National independence and sovereignty, multiplied and sanctified in the last decades, had not turned out to be a reliable road to a greater individual liberty and more secure international peace."

The Myth of Racialism. Racialism—the twin and *alter ego* of nationalism—emerged as a dynamic factor of intensity and importance in our times. It developed in the nineteenth century in the atmosphere of a rising nationalism and its concomitant romanticism, and it was stimulated by closer geographical contact and the spread of more uniform patterns of civilization in the twentieth century. No longer did it matter that the serious student of history, the honest ethnologist, the realistic sociologist, and the scholarly anthropologist regarded the pseudo-science of racial biology as the fantastic invention of mystics and romantics. The twentieth century saw racialism exerting a powerful influence in the economic and political struggles of nations, the ambitions of dictators, and the conflicts between classes.

The racialists used primitive superstitions to link race and class with blood. From the racialists' point of view, the rhythm of history as manifested in the rise and decline of civilizations may be explained on a purely racial basis: nations arise when a "superior" race conquers an inferior one, and they decline when the blood of the creative race runs thin through miscegenation with lower races. Race theorists held that the traits of ethnic groups are innate and are governed by immutable laws of heredity. They drew an analogy between the life cycle of the race and that of the individual, and falsely identified race with language.

The theories of the racialists were based upon intuitive rationalizations, and, consequently, were largely negated by their own inconsistencies and fallacies. The abuse of the word "race" to justify national or political ambitions gave it a nebulosity that tended to confuse scientists as well as educated laymen. Race was used as a synonym for people, nationality, language, or group customs. There never was, nor is there today, a German *race*, but a German *nation;* there is no Aryan *race*, but there are Aryan *languages;* there was no Roman *race*, but a Roman *civilization.*

Although used loosely to indicate groups of men differing in appearance, culture, or language, the term race in the scientific sense should be applied only to biological groupings of human types. It expresses the continuity of a physical type, representing an essentially natural grouping, and has nothing in common with the nationality, languages, or customs of historically developed social groups. The efforts of scientists to arrange the peoples of the world into some ordered racial classification have been hampered by the fact that distinct lines of demarcation do not exist. The first attemps to classify races on the basis of simple biological differences were inconclusive. Equally unsatisfactory were the attempted classifications by geography (common characteristics of populations in given areas), by history (migrations of peoples), and by culture ("racial mentality") derived from cultural conditions. With the development of anthropology in the nineteenth century came the introduction of quantitative methods of distinguishing between ethnic groups, an approach that at first seemed productive, but which later gave room for strong criticism.

The idea of "racial purity" has been effectively demolished by competent scientists. The various peoples of the world have become so intermingled that there is scarcely any possibility of the existence of a pure race anywhere. Leading ethnologists, without any important exceptions, agree that the juxtaposition of races has resulted in an extricable tangle of ethnic strains in which it is wholly impossible to distinguish a pure race. We are all energetic mongrels. Equally as fallacious was the myth of racial superiority. Based on the primitive fear and scorn of the unfamiliar, this theory was an irrational expression of the instinct for self-preservation. In a world of chaotic conflict, individuals and nations, like animals, tended to look upon strangers as natural enemies.

It thus became a matter of great importance to build up a sense of superiority. Critics of this doctrine point out that racial intermixture almost invariably produced a healthier stock and a more highly developed culture and that the intermingling of ethnic strains leads civilization to a higher plane.

Development of Racialism. As a political and cultural movement, racialism in its modern form developed since the period of the French Revolution. In the early nineteenth century, the discoveries of philologists led to the identification of race with language and to the belief that groups speaking the same language were descended from common ancestors. Chauvinists and super-patriots began to claim racial superiority of their own people and to disparage the heritage of other nations. The whole complexity of history was reduced to a simple formula of race. In the outburst of nationalism that preceded World War I, as manifested by Germany's drive for a place in the sun, Great Britain's Anglo-Saxon mission, and the demand of small states for national autonomy, racialism gathered increasing momentum. The map of Europe was remade at Versailles according to so-called "ethnic realities." "Racial minorities" sought President Wilson's intervention on the basis of "racial" (probably meaning cultural or linguistic) identity. Small nations striving for independence began to speak of "the self-determination of racially intact peoples."

Although racialism made headway in most countries, it was particularly virulent in Germany, where a hopeless and miserable people had suffered an ignominious defeat. Hitler's establishment in Germany of racialism as the legal basis for the State conferred upon it a pragmatic political reality. The Nordic myth, which in the eyes of competent scientists was merely the ludicrous fantasy of Count Arthur de Gobineau (1816-1882), Houston Stewart Chamberlain (1855-1927), and other savants, became a pattern by which millions of Germans were compelled to shape their lives. In stormy, violent, and vulgar rhetoric Hitler in *Mein Kampf* proclaimed the ideology of racialism and condemned all of opposing opinion as liars and traitors to civilization. He insisted that history had shown with terrible clarity how each time Aryan blood had become mixed with that of racially inferior peoples, the result had been the end of the culture-sustaining race. According to Hitler, everything admirable on earth was the product of only a small number of nations, and, originally, perhaps of one single race—the Nordic. Defining history as a struggle to the death between the Aryan and Jewish "races," he inaugurated a campaign to exterminate the Jews as "the destroyers of culture."

— 3 —

THE FIRST WORLD WAR, 1914-1918

System of Secret Alliances.   "You can explain most wars very simply," said President Wilson in 1917, "but the explanation of this war is not simple. Its roots run deep into all the obscure soils of history." Conflicting national and economic conditions were responsible for feelings of suspicion, distrust, and insecurity among the nations of Europe during the several decades before 1914. The quest for security took the form of secret agreements among nations that considered themselves threatened by the same enemies. The great powers aligned themselves into two rival camps. The result was a war marking a turning point in modern history—the first stage in the decline of Europe, a continent that in the previous four centuries had conquered and industrialized the rest of the world.

Triple Alliance.   Following the three wars for national unification, Bismarck organized an involved system of alliances designed to maintain Germany's hegemony on the European scene. His purposes were

to isolate France, conciliate Great Britain, and keep
Russia as a friendly power. The Three Emperors' Conferences (1872-1878), followed by the Three Emperors'
League (1881-1887), aligned William I, Francis Joseph,
and Alexander II in a triple friendly understanding. In
1879 Bismarck concluded the Dual Alliance with Austria-Hungary, by which the signatories were bound to
assist one another in the event that either ally was
attacked by Russia. In case of attack by any other
power, each signatory was bound to maintain a benev-
olent neutrality. In 1882 Bismarck expanded the Dual
Alliance into the Triple Alliance including Italy. It was
agreed that if either Italy or Germany were attacked
by France, the others would come to the assistance of
the attacked power. Angered by the French seizure of
Tunis, Italy joined the alliance even though she had to
submerge a deep-rooted enmity toward Austria-Hungary. In 1887 Bismarck concluded the Reinsurance
Treaty with Russia without the knowledge of Austria-
Hungary and recognized the predominance of Russia in
the eastern Balkans. Bismarck was certain that no power
or combination of powers would dare attack this strong
system of alliances.

Triple Entente. The Triple Entente was formed as
a counterpoise to German hegemony in Europe. European powers outside the Bismarck system began to
forget their differences and joined one another to form a
balance against the Bismarckian treaty system. Isolated
France gradually managed to free herself from the net
the Iron Chancellor had woven around her. The anti-
Russian policy of Bismarck at the Congress of Berlin
(1878) drove autocratic Russia into the arms of democratic France. The Dual Alliance between Russia and
France (1891-1893, officially confirmed in 1894), provided that if France were attacked by Germany (or
Germany and Italy), Russia would assist France. The
latter, in turn, promised assistance if Russia were attacked by Germany or by Austria supported by Germany. Thus, four years after Bismarck's retirement, a
coalition against Germany was in existence. Britain and
France, disturbed by Germany's navalism, colonialism,
and militarism. composed their long-standing differences

and signed a treaty of mutual understanding in 1904. Similarly, fear of Germany drove England to the side of Russia, her erstwhile traditional enemy. In 1907 England and France concluded agreements transforming their Entente Cordiale into the Triple Entente (England, France, and Russia), which provided for mutual assistance of the three powers in the event of war with the Triple Alliance. Europe was now divided into two armed camps, each side warily testing the other for points of weakness.

Fundamental Causes. This system of secret alliances must be judged by considering the climate of opinion in which it was bred. The general atmosphere was one of distrust, suspicion, and fear. Nations began not only to watch one another but even came to expect war. There was no international force strong enough to settle the rising differences between nations. The system of alliances was the approved method of seeking security in a world endangered by the clash of imperial interests and the global struggle for markets, raw materials, and colonies. The vital force of nationalism was the key factor that swept Europe into war. Many national problems remained unsolved, including Italian desires for unredeemed provinces in Austria, Serbia's call for Bosnia-Herzegovina, and a host of similar demands. The great powers were convinced that national interests could be furthered only by force, and even small nations became involved in the armaments race.

Diplomatic Crises, 1905-1913. The most critical spots were in Morocco and the Balkans. William II, protesting against French economic domination of Morocco and demanding a place in the sun for Germany, landed at Tangier in 1905 and ostentatiously recognized the Sultan of Morocco as an independent monarch. It was agreed at the Algeciras Conference of 1906 that an open-door policy in Morocco would be maintained under some French supervision. Germany was convinced that she had nothing to gain at international conferences. In 1911 Germany again vehemently protested French domination of Morocco. Similarly, a series of crises in the Balkans in 1908, 1912, and 1913 aggravated what was already a tense situation. In 1908, in defiance of

Russia's pretensions in the Balkans, Austria-Hungary announced the annexation of Bosnia-Herzegovina. It had been agreed at the Congress of Berlin in 1878 that Austria-Hungary was to have only a protectorate over these Serbian provinces. Russia's protests went unheeded. In 1911 Italy seized the Turkish province of Tripoli. In the Balkan wars of 1912-1913, Serbia, Montenegro, Bulgaria, and Greece jointly made war on Turkey, "the sick man of Europe," and then went to war with one another over the spoils. Austrians and Serbians, Teutons, and Slavs now because deadly enemies in the Balkans.

Immediate Causes. By 1914 it had become clear that "peace was at the mercy of an accident." The people of Europe, lulled into a false sense of security by four decades of peace, went about their everyday affairs in happy ignorance of the storm clouds gathering over the continent. Each year there was a serious diplomatic crisis threatening to bring the interlocking alliances into war, but each time the foreign ministers blustered their way out of the trap, and the crisis passed. Without a long-range policy to maintain the peace, the harassed diplomats improvised temporary solutions, knowing well that the hour was approaching when nothing could be done to prevent a frightful clash of arms.

On June 28, 1914, Archduke Francis Ferdinand, heir to the throne of Austria-Hungary, was assassinated at Sarajevo, the capital of Bosnia, by a young Bosnian youth on behalf of the Serbian Union or Death society, a terrorist organization agitating against Austria. Austria-Hungary, through her foreign minister, Count Berchtold, seized the opportunity to re-assert Austrian supremacy in the Balkans by dispatching, on July 23, 1914, a severe ultimatum demanding, among other things, that Serbia submit to Austrian domination in her police and law courts. William II had already pledged that he would support Austria in whatever demands she made (the so-called blank check). The Serbs submitted a conciliatory reply within the forty-eight hours allowed them, accepting most of the demands except that calling for collaboration of Austrian officials in suppressing anti-Austrian propaganda. (*See Document No. 1.*) The Serbs also offered to submit the entire matter to the Hague

Permanent Court of Arbitration, but simultaneously they began mobilization.

No peaceful solution could be improvised for this new crisis. All efforts to localize the conflict were futile. When Austria-Hungary began mobilization, the Russians threatened a similar step the moment the Austrians invaded Serbia. In the fatalistic climate of 1914, mobilization meant war. When Germany inquired what England would do if a war were to begin, Sir Edward Grey, the British foreign minister, replied that England would do that which best served her interests. The oracle at Delphi could not have delivered a more dangerously ambiguous response. Grey further proposed a European conference to settle the crisis, but Germany declined on the ground that the quarrel could be localized. Austria, categorically refusing to accept the Serbian reply, declared war on July 28, 1914. Russia mobilized the next day. On August 1, Germany declared war on Russia, after demanding in vain that the Russians disarm. Germany declared war on France on August 3. Italy and Rumania, asserting that they would not take part in an offensive war, announced their neutrality.

On the evening of August 3, with Great Britain on the verge of war, Sir Edward Grey stood at the window of the Foreign Office in London, watching the lamps being lit in the dusk, and said: "The lamps are going out all over Europe; we shall not see them lit again in our liftetime."

Problem of War Guilt.   A voluminous literature has been produced in attempts to shoulder responsibility for the outbreak of World War I on particular nations. One group of historians (Bernadotte Schmitt, H. R. Trever-Roper) regards it as proved that the war of 1914 was caused by deliberate German aggression. These observers state that: 1. the German General Staff, the ultimate power inside Germany, was convinced that it represented the voice and interests of the German people, firmly advocated aggression, wanted war, and wanted it in August, 1914; 2. German militarists carefully laid the groundwork over a period of forty years for the conflict, even promoting successfully a gigantic capital levy unparalleled in European history; and 3. diplomatic errors were made by non-German as well as German statesmen, but these errors were ultimately irrelevant when compared with the German drive to war.

After 1919 a group of revisionists historians (Sidney B. Fay, Harry Elmer Barnes) presented the explanation that, while Germany made some moves that contributed to a war situation, she cannot be accused of deliberately plotting to bring the war about. It is false, they say, to paint Germany's prewar record as uniquely black, since her statesmen worked more effectively than others to avert the war, and they knew that war might place German progress, already attained by peaceful means, in jeopardy. The revisionists set the order of guilt for direct and immediate responsibility upon Serbia, France, and Russia, with the guilt equally divided; next, far below, Austria; and finally, England and Germany, in the order named. This point of view was most acceptable, of course, to German historians then in the midst of a thoroughly organized campaign, led by General von Wegerer of the German General Staff, to combat the *"Kriegsschuldlüge"* ("war-guilt lie").

A third approach holds that responsibility for the war of 1914 was equally distributed, and that the war was the fatal result of unresolved economic clashes, the morass of diplomatic squabbles and intrigues, national rivalries, sword rattling, and a psychologically unsound conception of security. Those who take this attitude do not have in mind the crisis of 1914, but rather the general cultural and institutional situation back of the July clash. Certainly, serious mistakes of judgment were made on all sides during the critical weeks. (*See Document No. 2.*) While explanations may differ as to which individuals were responsible for casting the final die in the tragedy of errors of 1914, most historians agree that the climate of opinion was dangerously receptive to war. Lloyd George, however, explained the catastrophe in these words: "The more one reads of the memoirs and books written in the various countries of what happened before August 1, 1914, the more one realizes that no one at the head of affairs quite meant war. It was something into which they glided, or rather staggered and stumbled."

Course of the War. The Allied nations outnumbered the Central Powers in military strength in 1914 by some 30,000,000 to 22,000,000 combatants. The German army, superbly organized and equipped, was trained to the minute. The British navy dominated the seas. Bismarck's description of England as a "water rat" and Germany as a "land rat" was to be put to a test. Immediately after her declaration of war on France, Germany started her forces on a power-drive through Belgium. The Von Schlieffen Plan, organized decades before for such an eventuality, was designed for a two-front war. The idea was to swing into France with lightning speed, take Paris, and then turn on Russia for complete annihilation. Pushing irresistibly ahead, the Germans were stopped at the First Battle of the Marne (September 6-14, 1914), when, at the critical moment, von Kluck dispatched part of his forces to the Eastern Front. The Allies now won a race to the sea, after which the opposing armies dug in on a five-hundred-mile front for the remainder of the war. In the East, Russian armies had meanwhile invaded East Prussia. During the last week of August, a huge Russian army was defeated at Tannenberg by German forces under Hindenburg and Ludendorff.

In 1915 the Western Front remained stabilized. British troops poured into France. Italy, promised her unredeemed territories around the Adriatic, deserted the Triple Alliance and declared war on Germany. In 1916 the Germans attempted a mass break-through at Verdun, where they were repulsed with tremendous loss of life on both sides. In the meantime, the British navy, seizing control of the seas, effectively blockaded Germany for the rest of the war despite the threat of Germany's submarines. The only major naval engagement of the war took place in May, 1916 at the Battle of Jutland. Both sides claimed victory, but the German fleet retired to Kiel and remained there for the rest of the war. The tide swung definitely to the Allied side when in April, 1917, the United States, resentful of Germany's policy of unrestricted submarine warfare, entered the war. (*See Document No. 3.*) American manpower, money, and resources, thrown into the balance at a time when the Central Powers were almost exhausted after three years of war, meant eventual victory for the Allies. In the Second Battle of the Marne (July-August, 1918), the Germans made a desperate attempt to win the war, but the Allied counter-attack successfully halted them again. The armies of the Central Powers began to disintegrate all over Europe. An armistice was signed on November 11, 1918.

Costs of World War I. The human and material losses of World War I, which lasted 1565 days, were staggering. Some 65,000,000 men were mobilized during the course of the conflict, out of which about 9,000,000 —one in seven—died in action or of wounds. Some 22,000,000—one in three—were disabled; 7,000,000 were permanently disabled. More than 5,000,000 men were reported missing. The estimated number of civilian deaths as a result of the war was in excess of the military casualties. The total real economic cost was nearly $400,000,000,000. According to the Carnegie Endowment for International Peace, this sum would have been sufficient to:

1. Provide every family in England, Ireland, Scotland, Belgium, Russia, the United States, Germany, Canada, and Australia with a $2,500 house on a $500 five-acre lot and furnish it with $1,000 worth of furniture;

2. Provide a $5,000,000 library and a $10,000,000 university for every community in those countries possessing a population of 20,000 or over;

3. Create a fund which, at five per-cent interest, would yield enough to pay $1,000 a year to 125,000 teachers and 125,000 nurses;

4. Leave a surplus enough to purchase every piece of property and all the wealth of both France and England.

These figures do not take into account the disruption of European economy, the wholesale crippling of soldiers and civilians, or the vast sums to be appropriated for generations in the form of pensions. Added to this were the irreconcilable hatreds engendered by the conflict.

Results of the War. Four great empires were laid low by the events of 1914-1918. The Russian, Austro-

Hungarian, and Turkish empires, all belonging essentially to Eastern Europe, and the German empire, with one foot in Eastern Europe and the other in Western Europe, crashed in ruins. The Europe that had dominated the world of 1900 was now a shambles, and there seemed to be no possibility of reviving its prewar power. The continent was temporarily swept bare as if a swarm of locusts had descended upon it. Crowns rolled in the gutter, ancient tyrannies were broken, the economic system was in general bankruptcy, and the people were exhausted and insecure. Human ethics and morality had taken a vicious beating.

Two world messiahs emerged from this era of decay. Leadership from a battered Europe seemed to be out of the question. On the day the Armistice was signed, President Wilson announced: "It will now be our fortunate duty to assist by example, by sober, friendly counsel, and by material aid in the establishment of a just democracy throughout the world." The American President gave new hope to despairing Europe and urged his people to assume the unaccustomed rôle of leadership in the attempt to rebuild the world on a democratic basis. From Soviet Russia came the voice of Nikolai Lenin, foremost of Bolshevik revolutionaries, proclaiming the International World Revolution and urging his followers to organize the whole world in one single community dominated by the proletariat. The Wilsonian ideal envisioned a world reorganized on a democratic basis; the Leninist faith called for all or nothing at all. There was no compromise between these two points of view which became solidified in the next four decades. These were to be frustrating decades, witnessing the paradox of a drift to world utopias and the concurrent intensification of nationalism.

— 4 —

THE PEACE CONFERENCE OF PARIS, 1919

Organization and Procedure. Representatives and experts of thirty-two victor nations met at Versailles on January 18, 1919 to mend a shattered world by making a new map and reducing the territorial chaos. The problem was to effect a reasonable peace settlement in the presence of conflicting national ambitions, imperialistic aims, demands of military leaders for strategic frontiers, afterwar bitterness, the Bolshevik threat, and the popular desire for reparations. Germany, Austria-Hungary, Turkey, and Bulgaria were not represented at the conference sessions.

The ·Council of Ten, consisting of the premiers and foreign ministers of the major victor powers, was abruptly whittled down to the Big Three when it proved to be too unwieldy. The dominating personality at the conference was the American President, Woodrow Wilson, who received an extraordinarily enthusiastic welcome in Europe as spokesman for the masses. Wilson was denounced by his enemies as an impractical idealist and an indifferent diplomat. Believing that the people shared his hatred of war, militarism, and the old diplomacy, he was determined to see that the world be purged of war by the creation of a League of Nations. Georges Clemenceau, the French spokesman, demanded gruffly that once and for all time France must be made safe from German attack. He expressed his contemptuous attitude toward Wilson in a fiery statement: "God Almighty had only Ten Points; Wilson has to have Fourteen!" David Lloyd George, the British delegate, had promised the British people in the elections of December 14, 1918 that he would work to "hang the Kaiser" and collect from Germany the costs of the war "shilling for shilling and ton for ton." The routine commissions and the plenary sessions discussed a host of problems, including the League of Nations, the security of France, reparations, disposition of the Saar Basin, the Polish question, Fiume, and the German colonies. In practice the opinions of the Big Three governed the solution of all major problems.

Fourteen Points versus Secret Treaties. On January 8, 1918, President Wilson issued a statement of Allied war aims since known as the Fourteen Points: 1. abolition of secret diplomacy and provision for "open covenants of peace"; 2. freedom of the seas; 3. removal of tariff barriers and provision for equality of trade; 4. reduction of armaments; 5. fair adjustment of colonial disputes; 6. evacuation of Russian territory; 7. restoration of Belgium; 8. evacuation of France, and return of Alsace-Lorraine; 9. readjustment of Italian frontiers along national lines; 10. self-determination for minority groups in Austria-Hungary; 11. restoration of Serbia, Montenegro, and Rumania, and adjustment of Balkan disputes; 12. self-determination for the subject nationalities in Turkey, and internationalization of the Dardanelles; 13. re-creation of the Polish nation; and 14. establishment of a League of Nations. Reluctantly accepted by the Allied powers, these Fourteen Points made a tremendous impression in war-weary Germany, weakening the morale of the people and leading them to believe that their estimate of a fair and equitable peace could be won.

At Versailles this idealistic program came into head-on conflict with the Secret Treaties, by which the Allied powers had agreed that Russia was to get Constantinople and the Straits, Italy was to obtain sections of *Italia Irredenta,* France was to be awarded Alsace-Lorraine, and other assignments were to be made. In 1917, after the November Revolution, the Bolsheviks published the Secret Treaties found in the Russian archives.

Territorial Provisions. By the Treaty of Versailles Germany lost an eighth of her land area, some 6,500,000 people, and all her colonies. She was required to relinquish Alsace-Lorraine to France; Eupen, Malmedy, and Moresnet to Belgium; some parts of Upper Silesia to Czechoslovakia and Poland by plebiscite; northern Schleswig to Denmark by plebiscite; Western Prussia and Posen to Poland; Danzig to the League of Nations under mandate; Memel to the Allies and later (1924) to Lithuania; Kiao-chau to Japan; and her remaining colonies to the major powers as mandates of the League of Nations.

Military and Naval Clauses. Germany was required to submit to Allied occupation of the Rhineland with provisions for gradual retirement. The German army was limited to 100,000 men, and conscription was abolished. The German navy was limited to 6 battleships, 6 light cruisers, 12 destroyers, and 12 torpedo boats, and no submarines were allowed. The German air force was eliminated. German manufacture of munitions was restricted, the use of poison gas was prohibited, and German fortifications along the North and Baltic Seas were ordered demolished. The German General Staff was abolished. William II and other leaders were to be tried before Allied tribunals as criminals against international peace.

Signing of the Treaty. On May 7, 1919, the peace treaty was presented to the German delegates assembled at the Hall of Mirrors in the Trianon Palace at Versailles, where, in 1871, the German Empire had been proclaimed by Bismarck. The Germans were given three weeks to reply. On May 29, the German delegation submitted 443 pages in reply to the 230-page draft of the treaty, listing their objections to what they called a Carthaginian Peace. The Allies, rejecting the German reply, gave Germany seven days to accept the slightly modified treaty under threat of invasion. The Germans reluctantly signed on June 23, 1919.

Parallel Treaties. In the meantime, work went ahead on a series of more than a dozen treaties to liquidate the war. The Treaties of Saint Germain and Trianon effected the partition of the Dual Monarchy and led to the Balkanization of Central Europe. The Treaty of Neuilly with Bulgaria and the Treaty of Trianon with Hungary also followed the general lines of that at Versailles. Turkey repudiated the Treaty of Sèvres, and under Mustapha Kemal and his Turkish Nationalists went to war against the Greeks, who had British aid.

Victorious, the Turks negotiated the Treaty of Lausanne in 1923, by which they maintained their ethnic frontiers, freedom from international bondage, and national independence.

Minority Treaties. Aware that all national aspirations could not be satisfied, the Allied statesmen sought to protect the rights of minority ethnic and religious groups. While they declined to follow the same policies in their own countries, they compelled Poland, Yugoslavia, Czechoslovakia, and Greece to sign treaties guaranteeing equal rights to all citizens, regardless of race, religion, or language. The supervision over minority rights was left to the League of Nations; only by a majority vote of the League Council could these rights be modified in any way. Several countries, notably Poland, complained that these treaties were subversive of their national sovereignty, since the pacts were said to encourage separatist movements.

Effect on Germany. By the Treaty of Versailles Germany lost her colonies, virtually all her investments abroad, 15.5 per cent of her arable land, 12 per cent of her live stock, nearly 10 per cent of her manufacturing plants, two-fifths of her coal reserves, nearly two-thirds of her iron ore, and more than half of her lead. Her navy was almost wiped out, and her merchant marine was reduced from 5,700,000 tons to fewer than 500,000 tons. The surrender of colonies meant the loss of access to rubber and oil supplies. During the postwar period, every political party in Germany from Right to Left denounced the treaty as the *Versaillesdiktat,* as a peace designed to destroy Germany. It meant little to the Germans that they had imposed still harsher terms on the Russians a year earlier.

Estimates of the Treaties. The Treaty of Versailles and the parallel treaties were described by critics as one-sided, replete with unstable compromises, and as containing the seeds of future conflict. They were the result, said the critics, of hatred, vengeance, and blindness. Defenders of the treaties said that it was too much to expect that better treaties could have been drawn up in the material and psychological atmosphere in which the treaty-makers worked. Although it was strongly attacked in its day, the conference at Versailles succeeded in signing a peace treaty with the principal enemy within six months and with the lesser enemies within eight. This should be contrasted with today's lack of treaties nearly a decade after World War II. The conference at Versailles drew up, in thirty-nine hours of committee meetings and two plenary sessions, a covenant for a world peace agency which, after World War II, required a special conference of over a thousand delegates meeting for two months at San Francisco. It should also be realized that the delegates at Versailles were handicapped by the fact that many new states had come into existence before the armistice, setting their frontiers and consolidating their positions. Any significant changes in this pattern could be made only through the use of force.

— 5 —

INTERNATIONAL RELATIONS, 1919-1933

Temper of Postwar World.   The critical task in the postwar world of 1919 was to achieve international order on a scene marked by discontent of the defeated powers, disillusionment of the victors, and an America retreating into isolation. The League of Nations was devised as an attempt to implement the century-old dream of humanitarians that a world without war was a possibility. "The Covenant we offer," said Wilson, "must be based primarily upon moral sanctions with resort to force only as a last necessity."

League of Nations. The League of Nations, brain-child of Jan Smuts, was designed as an agency for han-dling affairs of common concern to all nations. The Fourteenth of Wilson's famous points had suggested the formation of a general association of nations. The first twenty-six articles of the Treaty of Versailles embraced the Covenant or written constitution of the League of Nations. The Preamble read: "The High Contracting Parties, in order to promote international cooperation and to achieve international peace and security by the acceptance of obligations not to resort to war, by the prescription of open, just, and honorable relations be-tween nations, by the firm establishment of the under-standings of international law as the actual rule of conduct among Governments, and by the maintenance of justice and a scrupulous respect for all treaty obliga-tions in the dealings of organized peoples with one another, agree to this Covenant of the League of Na-tions." Membership in the League was reserved for the victor powers (Germany was accepted as a member in 1926, Russia in 1934). The League organization con-sisted of: 1. an Assembly, representing all the members, in which each member was entitled to three delegates but only one vote, and which conferred, advised, and deliberated, but did not legislate; 2. a Council, composed at first of nine members (five permanent, representing the great powers, and four nonpermanent, chosen by the Assembly), with authority to formulate plans for the reduction of armaments and mediate in international dis-putes; and 3. a permanent Secretariat, composed of a staff of civil servants to collect data, register treaties, and perform the secretarial work of the League. Supple-mentary organizations, such as the technical organization of the Economic and Financial Organization, and ad-visory committees, such as the Committee on Mandates, worked hand-in-hand with the League.

Functions of the League. Article 10 of the League Covenant provided for an agreement among the member nations "to respect and preserve as against external ag-gression the territorial integrity and existing political independence of all Members of the League." Article 16 provided that should a nation go to war without first accepting arbitration, all the other members agreed "immediately to subject it to the severance of all trade or financial relations." If the economic sanctions failed, the Council could recommend to the members what armaments they would contribute to punish the recalcitrant nation. Such decision had to be unanimous. (*See Document No. 4.*)

Handling of Political Disputes. The League handled more than thirty serious political disputes, most of them legacies of the war. Differences over the Aaland Islands in the Gulf of Bothnia between Finland and Sweden were settled by awarding the islands to Finland with the provision that she was to respect Swedish rights. The Mosul Boundary dispute was ended by fixing the boundary between Turkey and Iraq. The Corfu dispute between Italy and Greece was resolved by ordering Greece to pay an indemnity to Italy for the assassination of Italian diplomats on Greek soil. Similarly, disputes over Vilna, Memel, Upper Silesia, Albania, Chaco, and Leticia were arbitrated with more or less success. While settling relatively minor differences, the League failed to deal effectively with such major disputes as those arising over Japan's actions in Manchuria in 1931, the Italo-Ethiopian War, and the Spanish Civil War.

Administrative Work. The League sought to alleviate economic distress in Austria, Hungary, Greece, Bulgaria, Estonia, and Danzig but without much success in an era of general worldwide economic insecurity. It supervised the plebiscite of January 13, 1935, by which the Saar Basin was awarded to Germany. It administered Danzig until the Nazis obtained control of the city in 1939. Each year the League received reports on the mandates, the surrendered possessions of Germany and Turkey (*Class A mandates,* lands which had reached a comparatively high stage of development—Syria, Lebanon, Palestine, Transjordania, and Iraq; *Class B mandates,* lands which were less advanced—Cameroons, East Africa, Togoland, and Ruanda-Urundi; and *Class C mandates,* remote and backward areas—Western Samoa, Nauru, Southwest Africa, and former German Pacific Islands). At the same time the League sought to guard the rights of some 30,000,000 people scattered throughout Europe under the special minority treaties. Little could be done, however, except protest against the more flagrant violations of minority rights.

Estimate of the League. The importance of the League of Nations lay in the fact that it established a precedent for a world order. It was handicapped by the failure to include the defeated powers in the original membership list. A more severe difficulty was the abstention of the United States. In Volume VI, *Triumph and Tragedy,* of his history of the Second War, Winston Churchill claimed that the League of Nations was ruined by the failure of the United States to take an active rôle in its affairs. Other contributing factors to the seeming failure of the League were the survival of power diplomacy, the unwillingness of the major powers to disarm, and the fact that the Peace Treaties were not adjusted to new conditions. Nevertheless, with the adoption of the Covenant, the governments as well as the peoples of the world, perhaps unconsciously, emerged from the chaos of unrestricted national sovereignty, and established a modest beachhead on a higher level of a world society with a formal constitution. With all its limitations, the League was the first important step in a system of permanent, organized international coöperation.

International Labor Organization and World Court. Article 23 of the League Covenant provided for an autonomous International Labor Organization dedicated to the maintenance of "fair and humane conditions of labor for men, women, and children in all countries." The I.L.O., an integral part of the League of Nations despite its autonomous position, made recommendations for the improvement of working conditions throughout the world, promoted progressive labor legislation, and supported research on labor problems. Although the United States refused to join the League of Nations, she became affiliated with the I.L.O. in 1935. A separate protocol provided for the formation of a Permanent Court of International Justice, or World Court, consisting of 15 judges elected for a term of 9 years. Its purpose was "to hear and determine any dispute of an international character which the parties thereto submit to it," as well as to issue advisory opinions upon any dispute referred to it by the Council or the Assembly of the League of Nations. A court of law (unlike the Hague Court, which was a court of arbitration), the World Court rendered decisions based upon international law. Presidents Harding and Coolidge vainly made efforts to have the United States affiliate itself with the World Court as a member.

Problems of Reparations. Article 231 of the Treaty of Versailles was the famous war-guilt clause, to which the Germans objected bitterly. In effect, it placed moral responsibility on Germany for causing the war, the first time in history that the right of the conqueror was not considered as sufficient in itself. (*See Document No. 5.*) The controversy over war guilt was heated and embittered. On July 25, 1914, shortly before he was assassinated, Jean Jaurès, the French Socialist leader, said in his last speech: "In an hour so grave, so filled with perils for all of us, I am not going to look for responsibility. We have ours, and I testify before History, that we should have foreseen them. . . . The colonial politics of France, the political underhandedness of Russia, and the brutal will of Austria have contributed to create the horrible mess in which we find ourselves." Germans protested vociferously that they were not to blame for the war. Nevertheless, the victorious Allies insisted that Germany pay reparations to the hilt.

The Peace Conference at Versailles, while fixing categories of payment (pensions, allowances, etc.) did not set a total figure of reparations but called for a payment of 5 billion dollars on account. In July, 1920, the apportionment of the indemnity was fixed at the Spa Conference by Allied statesmen at France 52%, the British Empire 22%; Italy 10%, Belgium 8%; and others 8%. In January, 1921, the Supreme Council fixed the total at 55 billion dollars. In April, 1921, the Reparations Commission set the figure at 35 billions. By the London Agreement of May, 1921, the total was reduced to 16 billions. The inability and unwillingness of the Germans to meet the annual installments led to French occupation of the Ruhr in January, 1923. Germany soon underwent a crippling inflation and economic collapse.

The Dawes Plan (1924) was devised to balance Germany's budget and stabilize the mark. The recommendations of the Dawes Committee included: 1. a sliding scale of German payments for five years from 250 million dollars to 625 million dollars; 2. the funds were to be obtained from mortgages on German railways, industries, and a transport tax; 3. German currency was to be stabilized by means of a foreign loan; and 4. fiscal and economic unity were to be restored to Germany. The Dawes Plan failed because it did not set a total reparations bill and because Germany was still subjected to foreign international control.

In 1929 the Young Plan provided for: 1. a fixed capital value of reparations at 8 billion dollars payable in 58 annual installments; 2. identity of the number of installments with the number of interallied debt installments; and 3. provision for a Bank of International Settlements (B.I.S.) for handling all payments. The Young Plan was upset by the world depression of 1929. President Hoover in 1931 proposed a year's moratorium on war debts and reparations. The next year, by the Lausanne Settlement, Germany was required to make a final payment of 714 million dollars in bonds to the B.I.S., the bonds to be negotiated at the end of three years, while a Gentleman's Agreement was made making settlement contingent upon a satisfactory adjustment of war debts.

War Debts. The problem of reparations was closely linked with that of war debts. Debts owed to the United States totaled 10 billion dollars, to England 8¾ billions, to France 2 billions. American statesmen demanded the repayment of these debts as legitimate loans, while their European counterparts, pointing to America's increase in wealth during the war and the fact that she had entered the conflict late, urged cancellation. Funding agreements between the nations concerned provided for cancellations varying from 18 to 75 per cent, a decrease in interest rates, and payment in annual installments over a period of 62 years. Even the generous reduction of debts failed to solve the bitter differences of opinion. The outbreak of World War II merely suspended the controversy over the debts incurred in World War I.

6

THE QUEST FOR SECURITY AND DISARMAMENT

Climate of Opinion. The system of diplomatic alliances and the armaments race before World War I were not effective in forestalling conflict on a global scale. After 1919 little was learned from past experience as the nations of the world once again revived the futile behavior of the past in their quest for security and disarmament. The defeated powers, discontented with the peace settlements, did what they could to repudiate the agreements. Soviet Russia and the Western powers were mutually suspicious of one another, the French were depressed by a feeling of insecurity, and the British continued to think and act in terms of the old balance of power. The stage was set for an even greater conflict.

The League's Security System. In this highly dangerous situation the League sought to improve the security system it had organized. The draft Treaty of Mutual Assistance, unanimously adopted in September, 1923, called for member nations to aid one another if attacked and directed the League Council to determine the aggressor within four days after the outbreak of a dispute. This draft treaty was strongly criticized on the ground that the terms "aggressor" and "aggression" were not adequately defined. No nation signed the proposed treaty. England, especially, opposed the agreement because it called for global commitments that she was not prepared to undertake. In 1924, Eduard Herriot and Ramsay MacDonald proposed the Geneva Protocol, or the Protocol for the Pacific Settlement of International Disputes, which defined an aggressor as a member nation which resorted to war before employing some peaceful method of settling a dispute. (*See Document No. 10.*) This, too, proved futile. The British Conservative ministry, under

Prime Minister Stanley Baldwin, refused ratification, and the document never came into force.

Rival Alliances. Three systems of military alliances —French, Russian, and Italian—were set up almost immediately after World War I. France, with a passion for security amounting almost to a fixation, proposed immediately after the peace negotiations an Anglo-American Treaty of Guarantee designed to preserve her from a future attack by Germany, but the United States Senate refused to ratify the treaty and England was reluctant to give a unilateral guarantee. Unwilling to depend upon the League for security, the French concluded a series of alliances and alignments designed to assure their hegemony in Europe (Belgium, 1920; Poland, 1922; Czechoslovakia, 1924; Rumania, 1926; Yugoslavia, 1927; Russia, 1933, and England, 1938). In the meantime, France encouraged the formation of the Little Entente by Masaryk and Beneš in 1920 and 1921 between Czechoslovakia, Yugoslavia, and Rumania which was designed to prevent the restoration of Hapsburg dominions.

Fearing a combined international effort to destroy her communistic experiment, Russia concluded a chain of non-aggression pacts and commercial treaties with her neighbors (Germany, 1922; Turkey, 1925-1933; Lithuania, 1926; Afghanistan, 1926; Persia, 1927; Finland, 1931; Latvia, 1933; France, 1933; Poland, 1933; and Rumania, 1934).

Italy, disappointed by the peace treaties and eager to obtain Nice, Savoy, and areas of North Africa, similarly concluded a series of treaties of friendship and neutrality (Czechoslovakia, 1924; Yugoslavia, 1924; Rumania, 1926; Albania, 1927; Hungary, 1927; Turkey, 1928; Greece, 1928; and Germany, 1936 [Rome-Berlin Axis]).

These international agreements were expanded in a complicated maze of alignments. The Four Power Treaty (1933) between Italy, France, England, and Germany, was regarded by Soviet Russia as a new "Holy Alliance" directed against her. The Balkan Pact (1934), signed by Greece, Rumania, Turkey, and Yugoslavia, was designed to prevent Italian expansion in the Balkans. The Stresa Agreement (1935) sought to form a united front between Great Britain, France, and Italy. The balance of power shifted once more in 1936 with the formation of the Rome-Berlin Axis and again in 1939 with the Berlin-Moscow Axis.

Locarno Treaties (1925). The Rhineland still remained one of the danger spots of Europe. When Germany proposed frontier guarantees to France, Stresemann of Germany, Briand of France, and Austin Chamberlain of England met at the Locarno Conference in Switzerland (October 5-16, 1925) and drafted a series of seven treaties. The boundaries of Germany, France, and Belgium, as set by the peace treaties, were guaranteed; the signatories agreed to arbitrate all disputes; Germany renounced her claim to Alsace-Lorraine; France agreed to relinquish her efforts to establish a separatist republic in the Rhineland; and Germany was admitted to the League of Nations. There was much praise for the new Spirit of Locarno, which, it was believed, would lead to a new era of peace and good-will.

Kellogg-Briand Peace Pact (1928). The spirit of conciliation was again demonstrated in 1928 when the French petitioned the United States to enter into a pact mutually outlawing war. The United States then proposed a multilateral treaty, the Kellogg-Briand Peace Pact, or the Paris Peace Pact (August 27, 1928), by which the signatories of some fifteen nations agreed to renounce war as an instrument of national policy and subscribed to the principles of arbitration and conciliation to settle international disputes. By 1933 sixty-two nations signed the pact, but its failure to settle the Manchurian controversy in 1931 showed that something more than an international agreement was required to prevent war.

Problem of Disarmament. The desire of reasonable men to reduce or abolish the old competition in military and naval armaments was frustrated by the close link between security and disarmament. The Covenant of the League of Nations contained several provisions for disarmament, but they were never successfully implemented. In 1921-1922, President Harding called the Washington Naval Conference which, by a Five-Power Treaty, provided for a ten-year capital ship holiday and restricted the remaining ships to a ratio of United States, 5; Great Britain, 5; Japan, 3; France, 1.67; and Italy, 1.67. The Geneva Naval Parley, called in 1927 to limit the construction of smaller ships, broke up without any accomplishments. The London Naval Conference of 1930 agreed on a six-year agreement limiting the tonnage of cruisers and submarines, but its effect was destroyed by including an escalator clause permitting any signatory to increase its naval tonnage should it feel that any other country endangered its security. (*See Document No. 11.*) The London Naval Parley of 1935-1936 was called when Japan demanded naval equality with Great Britain and the United States. The result was that the Great Powers terminated the capital-ship holiday and resumed unlimited construction.

Attempts to achieve land disarmament were similarly unsuccessful in view of the lack of a common yardstick. The League strove valiantly to achieve a measure of disarmament but always without success. At the World Disarmament Conference, held at Geneva in 1932, various plans were proposed to surmount the difficulties. President Herbert Hoover suggested a one-third reduction in land forces and the total abolition of tanks, bombing planes, and large mobile guns. Germany insisted that she be permitted to arm to French parity, and after failure she left the Conference and resigned from the League (October, 1933). Further meetings in 1934 resulted only in hopeless deadlock, whereupon the Conference adjourned. The Conference having failed, all further efforts to limit armaments were abandoned.

7

NATIONALISM AND IMPERIALISM IN THE NEAR EAST AND FAR EAST

Turkish Republic. The Ottoman dynasty and the Muslim religion, which had dominated Turkish affairs for so long, were strongly affected by the war. The incompetence of the sultans and the nationalistic drives of the subject nationalities led to the emergence of a new Turkey. The Young Turks, educated in the West and anxious to transform Turkey into a modern parliamentary state, gradually organized a new state. Under the leadership of Mustapha Kemal (Ataturk), Turkish opinion was rallied around a nationalist program. The victory of Turkey at Lausanne was followed by the establishment of the Turkish Republic and the beginning of the Kemalist dictatorship, which secularized Turkish life, reoriented the nation's society along Western lines, and introduced a program of industrialization.

Egypt. Although she had been under British control since 1882, Egypt at the outbreak of World War I was technically Turkish territory. In 1914, however, the British freed Egypt from Turkey and proclaimed a protectorate. Turkey renounced all her rights to Egypt by the treaties of Sèvres and Lausanne. Dissatisfied with British control, Egyptian nationalists, or Wafdists, demanded political independence and the establishment of a republic. When the Lord Milner Report of 1919 did not provide for absolute independence, the Wafdists once more rose in rebellion. In 1922 the British protectorate was terminated, Egypt declared her independence, and Fuad I assumed the title of King. In bringing her protectorate to an end, England insisted upon the security of British Empire communications, control of the Sudan, and protection of foreign interests in Egypt. The Anglo-

Egyptian Treaty of 1936 provided for England's maintenance of military control of the Suez Canal, joint government of the Sudan by Egypt and England, abolition of capitulations and extraterritoriality in Egypt, and Egypt's entrance into the League of Nations under British sponsorship.

Syria-Lebanon. The French experienced great difficulties in governing the mandates of Syria and Lebanon, to the north of Palestine. Attempts were made to crush the desire for self-determination by introducing martial law. The League of Nations Mandates Commission protested the French use of air raids to subdue the rebellious Druses. Concessions to native nationalism were made when the French "made preparations" to grant independence to her mandate. In 1936 France concluded treaties of alliance and friendship with Syria and Lebanon, by which they were to be sponsored for League of Nations membership. The outbreak of World War II saw the 1936 treaties still unratified and widespread discontent in Syria and Lebanon. In 1941 Syria was proclaimed a republic by the Free-French forces.

Palestine. Palestine was established at the Peace Conference as a Class A mandate under the supervision of Great Britain. The Balfour Declaration of 1917, promising a national homeland for the Jews, was satisfactory neither to Jews nor Arabs. The British sought to retain control of Palestine not only because of its strategic position but also because the Mosul oil pipe line terminated at Haifa. The complicated situation was not helped by Sir Herbert Samuel's proposed constitution of 1922 nor by the Peel Report of 1936, both of which sought to resolve the triangular conflict between English, Arabs, and Jews. In the meantime, political Zionism called for an independent Palestine. The White Paper of 1939, envisaging the creation of an independent state of Palestine at the end of a ten-year period, was rejected categorically by the Zionists. In May, 1948, as the British brought their mandate to an end after interminable clashes in Palestine, the Zionists established the independent state of Israel with Chaim Weizmann as president and Ben Gurion as prime minister.

Far East. Following the report of the Simon

Commission in 1930 and a series of Round Table Conferences in 1930, 1931, and 1932, India was granted an autonomous, although not completely independent scheme of Government by the Government of India Act of 1935. In China, concessions were made at first to a rising nationalism by checking Japanese aims in China and by supporting the Kuomintang nationalist movement. In 1931 Japan occupied Manchuria on the Chinese mainland, created the "independent" puppet state of Manchukuo, and sought to extend Japanese control over North China. Japan excused her aggression by insisting that China had violated the Twenty-One Demands of 1915, which had stipulated that China was responsible for maintaining peace and order and was obliged to prevent the boycott of Japanese goods. The League of Nations, seeking to adjust the Japanese-Chinese dispute, sent a commission to investigate the matter. Japan rejected the Lytton Report of 1932 and its recommendation of direct negotiations to settle the differences. In 1933 Japan served notice that she was withdrawing from the League.

— 8 —

THE DEMOCRATIC WORLD OF THE TWENTIETH CENTURY: THE UNITED KINGDOM

Progress of Political Democracy. The great hope of the twentieth-century democratic world was to advance the gains in democracy initiated in the English Revolution of 1688, the American Revolution of 1776, and the French Revolution of 1789. At the opening of the new century popular rule was neither complete nor unchallenged. Progress was rapid in those countries where democracy had taken root and where the old distrust of the common man as a revolutionary had begun to disappear. The franchise was extended, and the woman suffrage movement, though slow in getting started, was successful in Britain (1918), in Germany (1919), and in the United States (1920). The democratic countries revised their bicameral system of legislation by stripping the upper houses of much of their legislative power. With the defeat of ruling dynasties in Germany, Austria-Hungary, Russia, and Turkey, most of the succession states became democratic republics. Monarchical Europe, with a thousand years of traditional ruling dynasties, was transformed into republican Europe, with only eight monarchies left in twenty-six states. In the Orient, despite relics of the old imperialism, democracy made a belated appearance, but its path was rugged. Gains in religious and educational equality were made in the democratic states throughout the world.

Political Developments. Great Britain, although on the winning side in World War I, found herself confronted in the postwar period with problems of chronic unemployment, declining foreign trade, and an unstable currency. The Lloyd George coalition (1916-1922) negotiated with the Irish, proposed reforms for India, and concluded a trade treaty with Soviet Russia in 1921. The cabinet fell on the issue of pro-Irish treatment, a weak foreign policy, and economic depression. The Conservative ministries of 1922-1924, promising "tranquillity and stability," sought to solve the financial difficulties by enacting higher protective tariffs and by placing lower duties on British imperial merchandise (imperial preference). The First Labour Ministry (January, 1924—November, 1924), headed by James Ramsay Mac-Donald, concluded the Dawes Plan, issued the Geneva Protocol, and recognized Soviet Russia, but it was defeated on the issue of Anglo-Soviet friendship. The Conservative Ministry (1924-1929) concluded the Locarno Pact (1925), sponsored German membership in the League of Nations, and severed diplomatic relations with Russia. This ministry fell on the issue of unemployment. The Second Labour Ministry (1929-1931) accepted the Young Plan, renewed relations with the Soviet Union, but failed to solve the unemployment problem. The National Coalition (1931-1935) abandoned the gold standard, supported the Disarmament Conference of 1932-1933, and called the World Economic Conference (1933). The Conservative Government of 1935 forced the resignation of Edward VIII, attempted to neutralize the Rome-Berlin Axis by concluding defensive alliances, and declared war on Germany (September 3, 1939).

Economic Policies. The English depression became chronic after World War I due to the burden of the national war debt, the economic rivalry of the United States and Japan, the use of obsolete machinery, the impoverishment of British customers, high tariffs, and the British persistence in remaining on the gold standard until 1931. Many attempts were made to solve the economic dilemma. The Lloyd George Coalition ministry enacted the Unemployment Insurance Act of 1920, increasing the dole and passed the Safeguarding of Industries Act which established a protective tariff of 33⅓%. The Conservative and Labour parties differed on the problem of free-trade versus protection, the former favoring higher protective tariffs, while the latter supported free-trade. Both parties extended the system of unemployment insurance and advocated widows', orphans', and old-age insurance. The Labour party proposed a capital levy on large fortunes and the nationalization of key industries, while the Conservatives saw a solution in higher income taxes and the reduction of salaries of governmental employees.

Religion and Education. The Anglican Church is the state church of England, and the sovereign is by law the supreme governor of the Church. Full religious liberty exists, and there are no civil disabilities because of religion. In 1919 the Church of England Assembly (Powers) Act was passed, designed to make the Church more self-governing, although Parliament still retained ultimate authority. In 1928 the new revised Prayer Book, prepared to bring the doctrines of the Anglican Church closer to those of the Roman Catholic Church, was rejected by the House of Commons mostly through the opposition of non-Anglican Protestants. In 1918 the Fisher Educational Act provided for a system of free, compulsory elementary education and scholarships for secondary education. The postwar years brought a great expansion of the British university system.

Irish Free State. For centuries there had been unremitting agitation in Ireland for freedom from Britain. The British, regarding an independent Ireland as a possible military base for their enemies, rigidly refused to grant independence. The 26 southern counties of Ireland, agricultural and Roman Catholic, loudly demanded freedom, while the six northern counties of Ulster, industrial and Protestant, preferred to retain their bonds with the Empire. At the beginning of World War I, the British Parliament enacted the Home Rule Bill of 1914, granting a large degree of autonomy to Ireland, but its operation was suspended because of the war. The Irish Home Rule Bill of 1920 set up two distinct governments, Northern Ireland and the Irish Free State. The Irish Constitution of 1937 made no mention of the King of England nor the British Commonwealth. Agitation continued for the return of Ulster.

British Commonwealth of Independent Nations. Since the great Imperial Conference of 1911, the slow political growth of dominion authority in Canada, Newfoundland, the Union of South Africa, Australia, and New Zealand had been sanctioned by England. In 1930 the Imperial Conference accepted the Balfour Report declaring Great Britain and her dominions to be autonomous communities within the British Empire, but that all were bound to the Crown by a common allegiance. These principles were expressed in the Statute of Westminster (1931), creating the British Commonwealth of Independent Nations and binding the nations in a Commonwealth citizenship.

THE UNITED STATES

Postwar America. The United States emerged from World War I the greatest political and economic power in the world. From 1790 to 1940 the population of the United States, a fusion of diverse peoples, increased more than thirty times rising from 3,929,214 to 131,-669,275. Today more than one-half the total manufactured products possessed by mankind is credited to the United States, as well as nearly one-half the total income of the world. On the domestic scene, the giant nation was absorbed with the problems of conserving natural resources and assuring social justice in a rapidly expanding economy. In foreign affairs, the nation had to face its new rôle of "manifest destiny" in world affairs, the pressing problem of relations with Asia, and the conflict of isolation versus world-leadership.

Second Presidency of Wilson (1917-1921). Wood-row Wilson had been reëlected in 1916 on the slogan, "He kept us out of war." Despite the triumph of 1918, the American people immediately reverted to their traditional policy of keeping out of foreign entanglements. The attitude was a contradictory one, since the United States had participated in every major European conflict from the eighteenth to the twentieth century. Although President Wilson made a zealous attempt to persuade the people of the United States to accept the Covenant of the League of Nations and the Versailles Treaty, he was unable to overcome the opposition of what he called "a little group of willful men," including Senators Henry Cabot Lodge, W. E. Borah, and Hiram Johnson. The most serious objection to the League concerned Article 10 of the Covenant which guaranteed the territorial integrity and political independence of all member nations and which, it was felt by isolationists, would mean that American troops would have to be sent to adjust any further quarrels in Europe. In November, 1919, and in March, 1920, the Senate rejected acceptance of the Covenant in any form, thereby, in effect, dooming the usefulness of the League.

Warren G. Harding (1921-1923). In the election of 1920 the Democrats were thrown out of power on the issues of the League, the Peace Treaty, the high cost of living, and the economic dislocation caused by closing of the war industries. Under President Warren G. Harding, who called for a return to normalcy, the Republican Congress repealed the excess profits tax and enacted higher protective tariff schedules. The Harding administration was blackened by exposure of graft and corruption in the Veterans Administration and in the leasing of government oil fields (Teapot Dome scandal). Harding's most important achievement in foreign affairs was the Washington Naval Conference (1921-1922) which attempted to limit naval armaments and to find solutions for problems in the Far East.

Calvin Coolidge (1923-1929). Vice-President Calvin Coolidge, who succeeded to the presidency upon Harding's death in 1923, was reëlected in 1924. The country now entered a period of prosperity, during which the national debt and personal income taxes were reduced. In foreign affairs the Coolidge administration was faced with the perplexing problems of international war debts, confiscation of American investments in Mexican mines and oil fields, a revolution in Nicaragua that led Coolidge to send American marines to protect treaty rights in that country, the furtherance of good-will in the Latin-American states, and the issues of the World Court and the League of Nations. Coolidge announced that "I do not choose to run" at the end of his second term.

Herbert Hoover (1929-1933). In the election of 1928 Herbert Hoover, the Republican candidate, was elected to the presidency on a platform of farm relief, economy in government, better international relations, and enforcement of prohibition. It soon became apparent that the greatest industrial nation in the world could not isolate itself economically. The short-lived postwar prosperity was followed by the stock-market crash of October 24, 1929, after which American trade and capital export declined precipitously. The Hoover administration attempted a series of moves to meet the depression: the Hawley-Smoot Tariff of 1930 further increased the rates on manufactured goods and agricultural products; the Glass-Steagal Act of 1932 sought to rehabilitate business by making it less difficult to obtain loans; and the Reconstruction Finance Corporation of 1932 made loans to financial enterprises in difficulties. The Federal Farm Board was created in 1929 to help the farmer by buying his surplus production. In foreign affairs the Hoover administration took part in the London Naval Conference of 1930 and the Disarmament Conference of 1932-1933. The Stimson Doctrine (1932), refusing to recognize any territorial changes brought about in violation of the Kellogg-Briand Peace Pact, was announced after Japan's invasion of Manchuria and her establishment of the puppet state of Manchukuo.

Franklin Roosevelt (1933-1945).   Franklin Delano Roosevelt, defeating Herbert Hoover for the presidency in 1932, took office in a period of the gravest economic depression in American history. Roosevelt launched a New Deal for the "forgotten man" and an extensive program of social reform. (*See Document No. 13.*) His purpose, bitterly criticized by *laissez-faire* Republicans, was to bring all business enterprises under stricter federal control, on the ground that the stock market collapse, the increasing bank failures, and huge unemployment had been brought about by bankers, promoters, and industrialists. Furthermore, Roosevelt sought to protect the little man from destitution as the business depression spread. The Democratic Congress passed legislation calling for relief for the unemployed, federal loans to banks, financial aid to farmers, a civil works program, a Social Security Act for the aged and indigent, and controlled inflation. The new acts came quickly: Emergency Bank Relief (March 9, 1933) provided for stringent bank control and the prohibition of exporting or hoarding gold; the Agricultural Adjustment Act (May 12, 1933) gave relief to the farmers by reducing the acreage of basic agricultural products; the Muscle Shoals-Tennessee Valley Act (May 18, 1933) provided for a great public works project; the National Industrial

Recovery Act (June 13, 1933) brought codes of fair competition and the regulation of production; and the Railroad Relief Act (June 10, 1933) rescued the railroads from bankruptcy. Prohibition was repealed; immediate employment was offered to young men in the Civilian Conservation Corps; and small home-owners were helped. These relief measures rapidly increased the federal debt, whereupon new taxes were introduced on corporation profits, income taxes, and amusements.

The swing was definitely towards governmental economic and social control. Employers and business men complained heatedly, but small farmers, city workers, and the middle class in general approved the New Deal reëlecting Roosevelt in 1936 and 1940 by imposing majorities. Roosevelt thus became the first American president to serve a third term. Roosevelt's unorthodox domestic policies were supplemented by a strong foreign policy stressing world coöperation, friendship with the Latin American countries, and rigid opposition to aggressive nationalism. The world situation was so critical that the Roosevelt administration was forced to extend its efforts to bridge the economic crisis into a broad program of national defense.

— 10 —

CANADA AND LATIN AMERICA

Dominion of Canada. Canada, a bridge between Great Britain and the United States, was an autonomous self-governing Dominion in the British Commonwealth of Independent Nations. Politically oriented toward Great Britain, Canada was geographically, economically, and culturally tied with the United States. A vast and richly endowed country, Canada became one of the leaders of world trade. It maintained a restrictive immigration policy, accepting immigrants slowly. The two main national groups, British and French, remained loyal to their respective European cultural heritages but were united in their devotion to the British Crown and in their traditional friendship for the United States.

Latin-American States. Economically retarded, Mexico was beset in the twentieth century with the problems of land reform and with the desire for curbing foreign economic infiltration. Government after government fell on the issue of solving the hacienda system introduced by the Spanish three centuries earlier. Attempts were made to solve the issue of foreign economic control by confiscation, repudiation, or refunding.

Most of the population of Brazil, the fourth largest country in area in the world, was centered along the narrow coastline, with the Brazilian hinterland forming the world's largest tropical forest. The country's progress was hindered by unsatisfactory transportation, lack of coal, backward electrification, an oppressive climate, and the prevalence of disease. Nevertheless, with millions of immigrants coming from the distressed areas of Europe, Brazil made significant strides in education, transportation, and the exploitation of her natural resources. She maintained a traditional policy of friendship with the United States.

The Argentine Republic, while retaining the outer forms of democracy, developed into a dictatorship in 1946 with the election of Juan Perón. The Argentine government took the lead among Latin-American countries in opposing the influence of the United States.

The Latin-American nations in general had a similar pattern of problems: mixed populations, inadequate transportation, poverty, disease, bad climate, political instability, and economic vulnerability. While accepting the protection of the Monroe Doctrine, they resented North American "interference" in their affairs. Some twenty-one Latin-American republics remained economically dependent on the United States without whose naval strength they would have been helpless. A series of conferences for hemisphere solidarity was designed to meet the problems of regional solidarity and hemispheric security. The Communist-infiltrated government of Guatemala was overthrown in July, 1954 after twelve days of civil war.

— 11 —

FRANCE IN THE TWENTIES AND THIRTIES

Political Developments. Having suffered huge losses in manpower, money, and natural resources, France after World War I set herself to the tasks of restoration, raising money to defray the costs, and achieving a system of national security. The Third French Republic was a centralized state, with a weak executive, a bicameral legislature, and a cabinet. Where party government was the rule in England, coalition or bloc government was the order in France. The multiplicity of political parties and the constant cabinet reshufflings (there were more than a hundred different ministries since 1875) made for an unstable government, although the French believed that stability was maintained by a continuing bureaucracy and by consistent political principles among the various parties. The *Union Sacreé* (1914-1919) functioned as a coalition cabinet during the war years under the leadership of Georges Clemenceau. The Bloc National (1919-1924) upheld the Treaty of Versailles, demanded severe punishment for Germany, resumed diplomatic relations with the Vatican, strongly opposed socialism, restored the dev-

astated areas of France, and organized the futile occupation of the Ruhr in 1923. The Left Bloc (1924-1926) introduced anti-clerical measures, sponsored stability of
the franc, accepted the Dawes Plan (1924), withdrew
French troops from the Ruhr, and helped negotiate the
Locarno Pact (1925). The National Union Ministry
(1926-1929) reformed the system of taxation, stabilized
the franc, refunded the national debt, and continued the
reconstruction of devastated areas of France.

From 1929 to 1935 there was widespread ministerial
instability in France reflecting the economic distress of
the period, fear of Germany, and internal unrest. The
Popular Front (1936-1938), composed of a coalition of
Radical Socialists, Socialists, and Communists, attempted
reform by enacting legislation favorable to the workers,
nationalizing the armament industry, reorganizing the
Bank of France, and increasing taxes. In the meantime,
it opposed such Fascist organizations as the *Croix de
Feu* and the *Action Française*. The Daladier Ministry
(1938-1940) suspended much legislation of the Popular
Front, sought to stimulate production for national defense, negotiated the Munich Pact with Germany (1938),
and declared war on Germany (September 3, 1939).

Economic Policies. Postwar France remained in
chronic financial distress, with a huge national war
debt, reconstruction costs, an ancient system of taxation,
and an inflated franc. Ministries emerged and fell on
the issue of inflation. The government was on the verge
of bankruptcy and revolution as one ministry after
another sought to balance the national budget and restore some measure of national prosperity. The critical
economic situation was aggravated by the World economic depression, the loss of tourist trade, the non-
payment of reparations by Germany, the persistence of
France in remaining on the gold standard, and a high
tariff policy. Added to these troubles was the strange
attitude of many Frenchmen who failed to see any
connection between the payment of taxes and national
prosperity.

Religious Policies. In 1901 and 1905 a growing
sense of secularization had led to the reduction of
religious orders in France, the closing of monasteries and

schools, and the nationalization of Church property. In 1921 diplomatic relations were resumed with the Vatican, and efforts were made by the rightist political parties to effect a reconciliation with the Church.

Alsace and Lorraine. The cession of Alsace and Lorraine to France by the Treaty of Versailles was followed almost immediately by disputes over religion, language, political rights, and economic policies. The effort to Gallicize the area by banning the German language was opposed in the provinces. A compromise solution allowed French to be taught exclusively in the first two years of a child's school life, and German instruction was permitted as a choice thereafter. German-speaking natives objected strenuously when they were ousted from positions in the civil service and the public utilities. An attempt to disestablish the Church in Alsace and Lorraine by the Left Bloc in 1924 was met with a strike. Again, a compromise solution called for attendance at the same lay schools, with religious instruction offered in separate religious schools. In 1925 Alsace and Lorraine were incorporated into the government of France and were governed from Paris until the Nazi invasion.

— 12 —

OTHER DEMOCRATIC STATES

The New Austria. The Treaty of Saint Germain dissolved the Dual Monarchy of Austria-Hungary which had been established by the *Ausgleich* of 1867. When a constituent assembly, convening in February, 1919, failed

to achieve an Austro-German union (*Anschluss*) because of French protests, a federal republican constitution was promulgated with a bicameral legislature and
Dr. Michael Hainisch as first president. Reduced to
one-quarter of her former size and with a population
now of only 6,680,000, Austria found it almost impossible to maintain an independent economic existence
except with financial aid arranged by the League of
Nations. The League Council in 1924 guaranteed a loan
of $131,690,000 for twenty years, subject to the super-
vision of a League Commissioner. There was unending
political dissension as Pan-Germanists, Social Democrats,
Christian Socialists, and Communists sought to obtain
political control. The country was torn into two opposing
forces, the Reds and the Blacks. The *Schutzbund,*
dominantly Socialist, was in bitter conflict with the
Heimwehr, representing the Pan-German, Fascist, agricultural, and religious interests. Engelbert Dollfuss, a
Christian Socialist, became Chancellor in May, 1932.

The advent of Hitler to power in 1933 created a new
menace for Austria, when the Nazis launched an aggressive program to bring about *Anschluss* between
Austria and Germany. For the time being, Mussolini's
intervention saved the political independence of Austria.
On September 21, 1933, Dollfuss suspended the Austrian
republican constitution and established a corporative
state under authoritarian leadership. In 1934, the Austrian Nazis, with the complicity of Nazi Germans,
staged an unsuccessful revolt. On July 25, 1934, Dollfuss
was assassinated by Austrian Nazis. In 1938, following
a stormy meeting with Hitler, Kurt Schuschnigg, the
Austrian Chancellor, was forced to appoint several pro-
Nazi ministers to his cabinet. Fearing the outcome of a
plebiscite ordered by Schuschnigg, Hitler invaded and
annexed Austria on March 12-15, 1938. Austria was
now formally incorporated into the German Reich following a Nazi plebiscite that obtained 99% affirmative
votes.

Czechoslovakia. The Republic of Czechoslovakia
was created out of the three former provinces of Bo-
hemia, Moravia, and Austrian Silesia, and the two former
Hungarian provinces of Slovakia and Ruthenia. Thomas

Masaryk and Eduard Beneš were the fathers of what turned out to be the most democratic state in Central Europe. The constitution provided for a confederated republic, a legislature consisting of a Senate and a Chamber of Deputies, and a President elected for seven years by both houses. From its birth the Czechoslovak Republic had such internal problems as differences with the Catholic Church because of the expropriation of Church lands; the confiscation of land from royalty and nobility; and minority problems (in a population of 14,000,000 people there were, in addition to Czechs and Slovaks, some 3,300,000 Germans, 760,000 Magyars, 480,000 Ruthenians, as well as Poles and Jews). The new republic was the most prosperous economically of the Succession States. Most of the old Austro-Hungarian industries were located in Czechoslovakia, and, although landlocked, the new nation negotiated a number of fruitful commercial treaties with other countries. Since their absorption of Austria was only a prelude to further expansion in Central Europe, the Nazis intensified their propaganda among the German minority in the Sudeten area. The Czech Government vainly offered a series of concessions, but it was apparent that Hitler would settle for nothing less than union with Germany. German troops occupied the Sudeten area after the Munich Agreement of 1938. Although Britain and France guaranteed her new frontiers, Czechoslovakia did not survive her amputation. Beneš resigned under pressure from Germany, and the Czech Government was reorganized along pro-Nazi lines. By March, 1939, Germany occupied the entire republic.

The Smaller States. The acquisition of Eupen, Malmedy, and Moresnet brought valuable timber and zinc resources to Belgium. King Albert, who had achieved great popularity in World War I, rebuilt his country and devalued the Belgian franc after having been given dictatorial powers in a severe financial crisis. The most persistent difficulty was the Flemish problem. The Flemish half of the population agitated for suffrage and linguistic reforms, most of which they obtained by the thirties.

Queen Wilhelmina, who had commenced her reign in the Netherlands as a ten-year-old girl in 1890, continued on the throne after World War I. The Dutch, traditionally friendly to political exiles, granted asylum to William II. With a well-administered government, a large supply of skilled labor, effective union organizations, and a wealthy colonial empire, the Netherlands prospered. The foreign policy was to preserve strict neutrality in the quarrels among the great powers.

The Treaty of Versailles forbade Luxemburg to continue as a member of the German tariff union. A tiny nation, Luxemburg faced the world with an army consisting of one company of volunteers with 170 men and 6 officers. It remained industrially strong due to its great iron deposits. Its influence on the international scene was negligible.

With a similar historical background, the three Scandinavian countries—Norway, Denmark, and Sweden—were progressive democracies with paternalistic governments and advanced systems of social insurance. All three operated on the basis of a capitalistic economy, somewhat modified by the widespread development of coöperatives. Educationally, the three countries remained at the head of the European states. Illiteracy was virtually unknown. All three states maintained a traditional neutrality and expressed their international mindedness by strongly supporting the League of Nations.

Established in a small country about half the size of Maine, the Swiss developed a reputation as the consistently neutral nation of Europe but, at the same time, imposed an obligation of personal military service on every Swiss male citizen from 20 to 48 years of age. Switzerland's system of democratic government was one of the most advanced in modern times. One of the most industrialized countries in Europe, Switzerland produced watches, precision instruments, laces, and pharmaceuticals. She became the most important financial center in the world. With an advanced educational system, full religious freedom, a tradition of political sanctuary, and a rigid policy of neutrality, the Swiss were among the most prosperous nations in Europe.

THE RISE OF TOTALITARIANISM

Failure of 1918. World War I left a legacy of unemployment, inflation, industrial dislocation, contracted markets, depression, and colonial unrest. The attempt by the have-not powers to achieve economic self-sufficiency in an age of economic dislocation led to their repudiation of liberal and democratic methods and the emergence of absolute and intolerant ideologies. Bewildered by the complexities of government and the stresses and strains of economic troubles, and not vigilant in encroachments on their liberty, the peoples of the have-not nations sought a quick solution to their problems by turning to the promises of dictators. There were certain common characteristics of postwar dictatorships, regardless of their official titles: 1. one leader became the symbol of the state with unchecked power to enforce his will; 2. propaganda, controlled by the goverment, was used to glorify the dictatorial régime, excoriate opponents, and mould the educational system to the whims of the leader; 3. all opposition was forcibly crushed, and failure to support the dominant party was considered to be equivalent to treason; 4. secret police and spies were utilized to cement the dictatorship; and 5. aggressive nationalism and militarism were promoted as a means of assuring the continued existence of the dictatorship.

Until World War I the term "revolution" had indicated a more definite advance of democracy toward individual freedom. After the war there appeared a new kind of revolutionary movement dedicated to the elimination of democratic ideas and practices. This totalitarianism took two forms—fascism and communism—both of which denied the freedom of the individual and established a new order elevating the state to an exalted position.

Despite its denial of the dignity of the individual, the

new totalitarianism obtained the support of millions and quickly became the most powerful and uncompromising enemy that democracy had known in its existence. The economic dislocations resulting from the war hit both the working and the middle classes. In some countries helpless and despairing workers turned to communism as a solution for their misery. In others, the middle class, hard hit by inflation, depression, and rapidly growing monopolistic combinations, accepted fascism because it promised to destroy communism and curb Big Business. The democratic countries maintaining the tradition of freedom of the individual were able to resist totalitarianism by inaugurating economic reforms. Others, notably Soviet Russia, Italy, Germany, Hungary, and Spain turned to communism or fascism as a solution for their ills.

— 14 —

SOVIET RUSSIA

March, 1917, Revolution. At the outbreak of World War I the entire Russian nation was swept by a wave of patriotic fervor. The spirit of the people began to break, however, under the weight of the prolonged struggle. There was much dissatisfaction with the inefficient and corrupt government, the incompetence of the military leaders, and the series of disasters that had overtaken the Russian armies. Famine was added to popular discontent; shops were looted; and strikes broke out among the transport and metal workers. In February, 1917, Nicholas II tried to crush a factory strike in

Petrograd and, on March 11, he dissolved the Duma. In the meantime, the workers had organized the Petrograd Soviet of Workers' and Soldiers' Deputies which, together with members of the dismissed Duma, led a revolution against the Czar and formed a Provisional Government headed by Prince Lvov, a moderate Constitutional Democrat (Cadet), and Alexander Kerensky. The Romanov dynasty ended when the Czar recognized the new government and abdicated. The Allies promptly recognized the Provisional Government.

Provisional Government. The Provisional Government granted full civil, political, and religious liberties, restored the constitution of Finland, granted self-government to Poland, and decided to continue the war against the Central Powers. The Lvov Cabinet and the Petrograd Soviet immediately began quarreling over the issue of continuing the war. The liberals were soon forced out of office, while Kerensky remained in the cabinet. Local governments fell into the hands of revolutionary councils, or soviets of workers', peasants', and soldiers' delegates who demanded immediate peace and the nationalization of all industries. The Bolshevik, or majority wing of the Social Democratic Party, opposing the Provisional Government as bourgeois, called for the extension of the revolution.

November, 1917, Revolution. At this critical moment the Germans, anxious to get Russia out of the war, sent Nikolai Lenin across Germany in a sealed train to Russia. Preaching the slogan of "Peace! Land! Bread!," understandable to the Russian masses, Lenin organized a *coup d'état* which was executed on November 6 and 7, 1917, just preceding the convocation of the second All-Russian Congress of Soviets. Lenin became chairman of the new Soviet of People's Commissars; Trotsky, who had played a leading rôle in the revolution, Commissar for Foreign Affairs; and Stalin, Commissar for Workers' and Peasants' Inspection. The Bolshevik government announced a program calling for immediate peace, suppression of all opposition, establishment of a dictatorship of the proletariat, and world revolution.

Treaty of Brest-Litovsk. As a means of exposing

"the capitalist, imperialist powers," the Bolsheviks immediately published the secret treaties of the Allies, to which the Czarist régime had subscribed. Trotsky suggested a peace based on self-determination, no annexations, and no indemnities, but the Allies ignored him. In March, 1918, the Bolsheviks signed a separate peace with Germany at Brest-Litovsk. Russia was obliged to surrender almost all the territory in Europe that she had obtained since the time of Peter the Great, pay 6,000,000,000 gold marks in reparations, and grant Germany the status of most-favored nation in Russian markets. The Treaty of Brest-Litovsk, an indication of what was in store for the Allies had they lost the war, was later abrogated by the victors' peace.

Consolidation of the Revolution. The Red Army, impelled by revolutionary fervor, was engaged from 1917 to 1920 in combating a series of counter-revolutionary movements led by former Czarist officers, adventurers, and representatives of the Allied nations. Aiming to revive the Eastern Front against Germany and to prevent the spread of Bolshevism, the Allies financed these counter-revolutionary attacks and blockaded Russia. The White invaders were ultimately expelled (1920) by Trotsky's Red Army, and the governments of Kolchak, Judenich, Denikin, and Wrangel collapsed one by one. At the same time, opposition to the Bolsheviks inside Russia was crushed by the Cheka, operating on the basis of terror and sending thousands of opponents before secret revolutionary tribunals. Nicholas and his family were exterminated in a cellar. The old nobility and the bourgeoisie, many of whom sided with the counter-revolutionary leaders, were stripped of their power.

Political Structure. The Union of Soviet Socialist Republics (U.S.S.R.) consisted of seven confederated socialist states, of which the Russian Socialist Federated Soviet Republic (R.S.F.S.R.) was the largest and most influential. In turn, these constituent republics were divided into some 2,500 political units. The federal state was declared to be "a free Socialist society of the working people of Russia." All the governments announced their belief in Communist ownership of the means of production to be effected through dictatorship of the proletariat with "complete authority" vested in the local soviets. The ballot was given to both sexes over eighteen years of age, provided that the voters were productive workers. Representation being vocational rather than geographic and indirect instead of direct, the higher authorities in the hierarchy were almost entirely removed from popular control.

Despite the window-dressing, the U.S.S.R. was in fact a dictatorship directed from above. Behind the elaborate and formal façade was the real power, the Communist Party, consisting of about 2,500,000 members in a population of more than 180,000,000, confined largely to the male population and to the city workers. The head of the party, the Secretary-General, exercised a political dictatorship through supreme control of the All-Union Communist Party. The Constitution of 1936 extended the seven constituent republics to eleven, abolished the All-Union Congress, simplified the structure of the state, established the Supreme Soviet, reformed the judiciary, issued a Soviet Bill or Rights, codified Marxist-Leninist-Stalinist principles and retained the basic Soviet ideology and the one-party system.

War Communism. From 1917 to 1921 the Bolsheviks in a surge of revolutionary fervor attempted to introduce pure communism throughout Russia. They abolished all private ownership of land without compensation; turned over the estates of the crown, nobility, and Church to district Soviets of Peasants' Deputies; and seized all factories, mines, railways, banks, shipyards, and natural resources. They forbade the ownership of private property, cancelled debts to foreign countries, and expropriated foreign investments in Russia. Chaos resulted as inexperienced party members attempted to run the factories and mines. The transportation system broke down and foreign trade almost disappeared. The peasants, resisting collectivization, hoarded their grain supplies. With production declining and a severe famine following a poor harvest, Russia was on the verge of a complete breakdown.

New Economic Policy. In 1921 Lenin recommended a New Economic Policy (N.E.P.), actually a temporary compromise with capitalism. Private retail trade was permitted under governmental regulation, small factories and shops were restored to their former owners, graduated wage scales were introduced, and experts were imported from abroad to manage the factories. In order to obtain liquid capital for the industrial development of the country, foreign capitalists were offered concessions for the exploitation of mines and oil wells. Finances were reorganized, inflation halted, and the currency stabilized on a gold basis. The system of requisitioning foodstuffs from the peasants was abandoned and a fixed tax on produce was substituted. The renewed opportunity for disposing of their surplus in the open market encouraged the peasants to enlarge their cultivable acreage. The government organized coöperative farming to bring about an increase in agricultural output. The result of these measures, "taking one step backward in order to take two forward," as Lenin expressed it, was that industry, business, and agriculture were brought back to prewar standards.

Five-Year Plans. The First Five-Year Plan (1928-1933) aimed at the complete industrialization of Russia. Under a State Planning Commission (*Gosplan*), production quotas were fixed, and plans were inaugurated for the rapid construction of new plants, factories, and mills for the operation of older enterprises at higher speed and for special efforts in the chemical, coal, oil, and similar industries. The goal was to increase manufacturing about 130% and agriculture about 50%. While some of the objectives were achieved, the quality of the output remained poor, and the inefficient transportation system hindered the distribution of manufactured goods. Some three-fourths of the arable land was collectivized. The Second Five-Year Plan (1933-1938) sought to eliminate the "exploitation of man by man" by improving the quality of consumers' goods, promoting collective farming by liquidating the *kulaks* (landowning peasants) and *Nepmen* (small businessmen), and establishing new industrial centers. The Third Five-Year Plan (1938-1942) called for the complete socialization of industry and the collectivization of farming. The Stakhanov movement, introduced at this time, attempted to substitute "socialist competition" for capitalist initiative by rewarding workers who produced above the norm in their factory or mine work. The Third Five-Year Plan was suddenly converted into a munitions production program when World War II began.

Social Life. The educational system of the Soviet Union attacked illiteracy, promoted experiments in progressive education, and emphasized the construction of technical schools. Great importance was attached to education, not only to combat the widespread ignorance among the masses but also to infuse the younger generation with loyalty to the Communist régime. In addition to the schools, every phase of national life was moulded by propaganda to conform with Leninist-Stalinist ideology. On the assumption that organized religion was an opiate of the people, the Russian Orthodox Church was disestablished, its property confiscated, and its churches converted to use as museums. Godless societies were encouraged, on the ground that religion and counter-revolution went hand-in-hand. Marriage and divorce were removed from ecclesiastical supervision and placed under civil control. The legal system and criminal codes were reformed in accordance with Communist doctrine. Prostitution and crime were treated as illnesses, with the death penalty reserved for the "true criminals—the enemies of the State."

Stalin versus Trotsky. A bitter struggle for power took place between Stalin and Trotsky after the death of Lenin in 1924. Stalin advocated a policy of socialism in one country; Trotsky demanded a permanent world revolution. This battle for political supremacy was won by Stalin, who thereupon proceeded to consolidate his own power ruthlessly by removing any opponents or possible enemies from the scene. Exiled from Russia, Trotsky, who had proposed the organization of a Fourth International, was assassinated in Mexico in 1940.

Foreign Policy. The foreign policy of the Soviet Union was based on the idea that the entire world was in deadly opposition to Russia. When the global revolution failed to materialize, Russia entered upon more or less normal relations with the capitalist nations. In 1922 she won *de facto* recognition at the Conference of

Genoa, and at the same time concluded the Treaty of Rapallo with Germany. When Britain recognized Soviet Russia in 1924, there ensued a worldwide movement to accept the new state as a member of the family of nations. Soviet Russia was admitted to the League of Nations in 1934. Between 1922 and 1938 she negotiated a series of trade, non-aggression, and neutrality treaties with her neighbors, while, at the same time, building a powerful army. In 1939 she abandoned her doctrine of collective security (full coöperation with the world democracies against fascism) and adopted a policy of aggressive expansion in Finland, the Baltic states, and Poland. Accusing Great Britain and the Western democracies of favoring Germany's drive to the East, Soviet Russia in 1939 concluded a pact with Germany. Hitler, believing himself secured against a two-front war, turned his armies westward. On June 22, 1941, the Nazi *Fuehrer* suddenly turned on Russia.

Estimate of Soviet Communism. Lenin sought to create a monolithic world of one faith and one leadership. This was the only kind of society, he believed, that could bring security to itself as well as salvation for the whole of mankind. Only if the enemies of the true faith were liquidated could there be a safe and secure world. To achieve this aim Soviet Russia fashioned a completely closed society, in which there was to be no opposition to the régime. Western ideas of liberalism and democracy were scornfully cast aside as inadequate by men who were convinced that they were wielding the sword of history. The task of enforcing absolute obedience was entrusted to the dread GPU (later the NKVD and the MVD), the secret police that held unlimited power over Soviet citizens. No one could be certain that his neighbor was not a member of the GPU. The result was a general spirit of distrust and suspicion.

The Soviet Union contributed a new kind of morality —anything was desirable if it was in the interest of the revolution. (*See Document No. 8.*) Millions of peasants starved to death in the early twenties when Lenin's grain collectors took bread from them by force. In the thirties Stalin's agents took the land as well as the bread, exterminating those *kulaks* who resisted. When Winston

Churchill later asked Stalin how many had been "blotted out or displaced forever," the latter replied, as recorded in Churchill's memoirs: " 'Ten million,' he said, holding up his hands. 'It was fearful. For years it lasted. . . . It was all very bad and difficult—but necessary.' "

At the same time a novel Aesopian language was invented—the distinctly undemocratic society of Soviet Russia was termed "a people's democracy." The aim supposedly was to establish a democratic society by the path of a totalitarian dictatorship. Class rule was abolished in favor of a ruling *political* class, something unique in history. The state was made identical and coextensive with society. Everyone had to do what the government prescribed. This repudiation of democracy was termed by Bolshevik logic "the new democracy."

Perhaps the best way to judge the Soviet state is to compare promise with performance. Marx described the revolutionary period between capitalist and Communist society as "nothing but the dictatorship of the proletariat." In reality, the Soviet Union was a dictatorship *over* the proletariat and not *of* it. The Central Committee of the Communist Party today comprising the "collective leadership" of the state is said to represent the best elements of Soviet society; not one of this group of 125 persons is a member of the Soviet proletariat. Engels predicted that under Communist society the state would wither away as a repressive force.

The Soviet Union today is probably the most repressive force in history; its leaders maintain that it must be strengthened ceaselessly as a means of defending socialism from foreign attack. Communist theology speaks of the Soviet Union as a democracy for the proletariat, *i.e.,* democracy for all. In fact, there is no difference of political opinion; the Communist Party is the only political party allowed to exist and all candidates for office must have the approval of the party. There is no freedom for cultural expression in the Soviet police state. Lenin preached the doctrine of equality—equality of wages, equality of labor, equality of human beings, and visualized the day when the maxim could be applied: "From each according to his ability; to each according to his needs." His admonition received little attention in contemporary Russia. Actually, a new privileged class has arisen consisting of the ruling Government officials, successful authors and entertainers, and top members of the Communist Party. At the other end of the scale is a mass of peasants and unskilled workers, whose standard of living is shockingly low. Though economic progress has been made, it was purchased at the cost of millions who died of hunger and in slave-labor camps. The Soviet Union today is a far cry from the Utopian society predicted by Marx and Engels.

— 15 —

FASCIST ITALY

Postwar Italy. Italian patriots, grievously disappointed by the Treaty of Versailles, demanded that their claims to Dalmatia and Albania be recognized, pleading that possession of these areas was essential to the establishment of Italian control over the Adriatic. The government was condemned for its failure to acquire colonial spoils in the Near East and Africa. The domestic situation in postwar Italy was critical: a shortage of food and raw materials, a rapid increase in the cost of living, an unbalanced budget, and currency inflation. Revolutionary activities were encouraged by the desperate plight of the masses. Following the example of Bolshevik Russia, Italian workingmen resorted to direct action by seizing factories and expelling the owners. An epidemic of strikes disorganized industry and essential public services. Serious disorders broke out in agricultural districts, where peasants seized the land, burned houses, and destroyed crops. The government, paralyzed by factional intrigues, seemed powerless. The country was ripe for revolution. It was at this juncture that the Fascist counter-revolution was set into motion.

Origins of Fascism. Benito Mussolini (1883-1945) had been a zealous Socialist in his early days. In World War I he was ousted from the party when he demanded that Italy renounce her neutrality and join the Allies. Later, as editor of *Il Popolo d'Italia,* he advocated a program of virulent nationalism designed to appeal to all his compatriots suffering from postwar discontent. Mussolini portrayed fascism as a politico-religious conception. (*See Document No. 12.*) Soon dissatisfied ex-soldiers, the depressed middle class, patriotic youths, hungry farmers, and radical intellectuals were organized into a compact political party, the Fascists (the name was derived from the Latin *fasces,* a bundle of rods encircling an axe, used in ancient Rome as a symbol of authority). Fascism, portrayed as a unifying factor that would save Italy from Bolshevism, gradually pervaded the bureaucracy, the police, the courts, and the army. Semi-military bands of Black Shirts began breaking up Socialist headquarters, attacking Communist meetings, and compelling workers to return to their jobs. Guns, clubs, and castor oil were used to make converts. The Fascists were victorious in the savage warfare in the streets—a virtual civil war. The triumph of fascism became inevitable when wealthy businessmen and industrialists rallied to its support. On October 26, 1922, some 50,000 Fascists marched on Rome, while Mussolini went in the same direction in a *wagon lit.* He intimidated the Chamber of Deputies and forced the resignation of Premier Facta. Several days later Victor Emmanuel made Mussolini premier.

Mussolini's Dictatorship. Within a year Mussolini transformed the Italian government, which had been modeled upon that of England, into a dictatorship. Rejecting democratic institutions, he demanded and received permanent control over all the military, air, and naval forces as well as the conduct of foreign affairs.

He was given the authority to create legislation by decree. Declaring that there was no room in Italy for any opposition, he suspended civil rights and discouraged his political enemies by imprisoning or exiling their leaders. Giacomo Matteotti, head of the Socialist Party, was found murdered, whereupon the Socialists seceded from the Chamber in protest. Mussolini further silenced criticism by establishing a rigid censorship, suppressing opposition newspapers, forbidding public meetings, dismissing university professors, and establishing special military tribunals to try all opponents of the régime. The Acerbo Election law, enacted in December, 1923, provided that the party polling a plurality vote in a national election was to have two-thirds of the seats in the Chamber of Deputies. With this contemptuous rejection of popular sovereignty Mussolini solidified his dictatorship.

Fascist Party. The Fascist Party consisted of: 1. the Grand Council of some twenty members, which drafted new legislation, filled its own vacancies, appointed the ministers, and named members of the National Directory; 2. the National Directory composed of the Secretary-General of the party and nine members with Mussolini at their head; and 3. such auxiliary organizations as the *Balilla,* boys from 8 to 14; the *Avanguardia,* from 14 to 18; and the *Giovani Fascisti,* from 18-21; and the Fascist Militia, or Black Shirts, for which military service was compulsory. Mussolini sought to satisfy the Italian thirst for the theatrical and the spectacular by demanding use of the Roman salute, colorful parades, distinctive uniforms, and the Fascist hymn, *Giovinezza.* (*See Document No. 7.*)

Corporate State. In originating the ideology of fascism, Mussolini had been influenced by the views of the syndicalist Georges Sorel who had repudiated the state, denounced capitalism, and demanded that the syndicalist state governed by trade unions be brought about by direct action and the general strike. In 1919 Edmondo Rossoni combined syndicalism with fascism and organized the Fascist Syndicates which defended private property, opposed class war, championed class collaboration, and supported integral nationalism. In

1926 Mussolini placed the vast organization of Fascist Syndicates under his own control. There were to be no strikes, lockouts, nor class warfare, but, instead, class discipline, absolute obedience, and "the sacrifice of the individual for society." Wages, hours, and conditions of work were to be regulated by a National Council of Corporations. A Charter of Labor, enacted on April 21, 1927, proclaimed: 1. higher pay for night workers; 2. an annual paid vacation; 3. no labor on Sundays; 4. social services to be provided by the government; and 5. free vocational education. In 1928 representation in government was placed on social status instead of geographic division. The right of suffrage was restricted to males.

Domestic Affairs.   On the assumption that his people were apathetic and undisciplined, Mussolini introduced a series of reforms. He drastically revised the system of taxation and finance, refunded foreign debts, and stabilized the currency. He enacted high tariffs, expanded the merchant marine, and concluded trade pacts with foreign countries. His extensive program of public works was designed to increase employment. He encouraged foreign capitalists to invest their funds in Italy, and began a campaign to attract tourists. He reorganized the educational system in an effort to combat illiteracy. By means of bonuses and tax exemptions, he encouraged large families, on the assumption that the future of Italy depended upon a great empire housing her excess population. He banned birth control, divorce, and emigration. The power-hungry dictator attempted to give his people everything except the one thing without which human life becomes meaningless—freedom.

Roman 'Question.   Subsequent to the unification of Italy in 1870 the Church persistently refused to recognize the loss of the Papal States. As a means of resolving the Roman Question, Mussolini, on February 11, 1929, concluded with Pope Pius XI a Treaty and Concordat, by which the absolute sovereignty of the Pope in the small Vatican City State was recognized in exchange for papal recognition of the Kingdom of Italy. Roman Catholicism was decreed to be the State religion. The papacy was reimbursed by a large indemnity, partly in cash and partly in State bonds. In July, 1929, Pope Pius

XI emerged into the Square of St. Peter's as a signal for
the settlement of the Roman Question.

Foreign Policy. The fervent exaltation of nationalism was a cardinal tenet of Mussolini's dictatorship.
The goal of Italy's foreign policy was to expand the
colonial empire to provide outlets for surplus population
and to obtain raw materials. The Adriatic and eventually
the entire Mediterranean were to become an Italian
lake (*Mare Nostrum*). Mussolini concluded a series of
non-aggression and friendship treaties with the Central
and Eastern Powers. His designs on Corsica, Savoy,
Nice, and Tunis enraged the French. Seizing upon a
boundary dispute between Ethiopia and Italian Somali-
land, Fascist Italy, in October, 1935, invaded Ethiopia
and annexed it despite stubborn Ethiopian resistance
and sanctions imposed upon Italy by the League of
Nations. In 1936 the Italian dictator aligned himself
with Hitler in the Rome-Berlin Axis in the belief that
the future belonged to the Fascist have-not powers.
Italian support for the insurgent cause in the Spanish
Civil War was an important factor in Franco's victory.
In 1940-1941 the myth of Italian military strength,
blown to enormous proportions by Mussolini's boasts,
was shattered on the sands of Libya before British tanks
and in Albania before Greek bayonets.

Estimate of Italian Fascism. Twenty-three years
of Fascism demonstrated effectively that Mussolini was
operating in the wrong century. Italy's geographic position, the hard core of the old Roman Empire, was out-
dated in the twentieth century, when it became merely
a peninsula locked in the Mediterranean. The Fascist
philosophy in action had little to recommend it. The
motto—"*Credere, obbedire, combattere*" ("believe, obey,
fight")—was not suited to the Italian temperament.
Rejecting individualism and accepting the Hegelian
dogma of the state as an ethical whole, Mussolini sought
to mould an entire people in his own image. He denounced democracy as a "putrescent corpse," insisted
that the masses were incapable of governing themselves,
demanded a new élite, and glorified war. The Italian
people learned about the effects of this philosophy the
hard way. Instead of lifting Italy to new heights of

glory, the egocentric dictator was responsible for her descent into defeat and misery.

— 16 —

GERMANY: *FROM THE WEIMAR REPUBLIC TO NAZI TOTALITARIANISM*

German Revolution. At the outbreak of World War I all political parties, including the Social Democrats, convinced that Germany's opponents had plotted her destruction, sprang to the defense of the Fatherland. As the war dragged on and the people suffered increasing hardships, distress and disillusionment began to undermine national unity. Many workers went on strike, and the sailors at Kiel mutinied. A coalition government, headed by Prince Max of Baden, converted the German Empire into a weak, limited monarchy, but President Wilson refused to deal with any other than a popular government. On October 23, 1918, William II fled to Spa. On November 9, 1918, the imperial régime yielded as Friedrich Ebert and the Majority Socialists took over controlling power from Prince Max. The Emperor abdicated and fled to Holland.

While ejecting the Kaiser and twenty-five sovereigns of the German states and proclaiming Germany a republic, the country was still burdened by the old socio-economic order. A federation of republican states, temporarily headed by a Council of Six People's Commissars (three Majority Socialists and three Independent

Socialists) was set up under the joint chairmanship of
Ebert and Haase. The Independent Socialists bolted,
whereupon the Majority Socialists took over. The Spar-
tacists, the Communist party, sought to extend the
revolution into a dictatorship of the proletariat, but the
Social Democrats, with the assistance of Gustav Noske,
crushed them, in the course of which Karl Liebknecht
and Rosa Luxemburg, Spartacist leaders, were killed.

Weimar Constitution. The political system set up
by the Weimar Constitution was pieced together from
the American, British, French, and Swiss forms of
government. Germany was to be a democratic republic,
with universal suffrage for all citizens over twenty years
of age. The Constitution provided for a President elected
by direct vote of the people for a term of seven years,
after which he was eligible for reëlection. Actual executive authority was vested in a ministry headed by the
Chancellor, appointed by the President, but responsible
to the Reichstag. The Reichstag, elected for a period of
four years, had the power of initiating bills. The old
Reichsrat, representing the states, was retained, but it
was now a secondary importance. A comprehensive bill
of rights insured the legal equality of the sexes, established free and compulsory education up to the age of
eighteen, and provided for a system of social legislation.
On paper the Weimar Constitution was one of the most
advanced in the history of mankind, but its value was
almost destroyed by Article 48, which permitted the
President to lift the entire bill of rights in emergencies.
(*See Document No. 6.*)

Trials of the Republic. The Weimar Republic was
burdened from its very beginning with an overwhelming
combination of problems: the bitter humiliation of
defeat, the currency debacle, reparations, and acute
economic distress. Not only were the German people ill-
prepared for an advanced form of democracy, but the
victor powers, which had once carefully distinguished
between the German people and their rulers, now
showed little sympathy or understanding for the fledgling
republic.

The new German government had to fight for its
existence against determined opposition from both left

and right. In 1919 the Communists were held in check by ruthless suppression. On March 13-17, 1920, the Monarchists, including Junkers, Pan-Germanists, and militarists, organized the Steel Helmets and the League of the Upright and sought to overthrow the government by marching on Berlin. This Kapp Putsch failed when a general strike was called. On November 8-11, 1923 Adolf Hitler and General Erich Ludendorff attempted a putsch in Munich (the beer-hall rebellion), but the movement was dissipated and Hitler sent to prison. A Rhineland Republic was established, but it was short-lived because of differences among the leaders and British opposition. The German currency inflation of 1923 reduced most of the middle class to poverty. The critical economic conditions made for political instability, as one coalition after another sought unsuccessfully to cope with the many problems. Public sentiment gradually shifted from a lukewarm liberalism to extreme conservatism.

Adolf Hitler.   The pivot around which the revolutionary movement revolved was Adolf Hitler, who was born in the Austrian village of Braunau on April 20, 1889, the son of a minor customs official. Imbibing a passionate German nationalism from his teachers, he moved to Vienna in 1907, where he led a precarious existence by selling postcards and working at such odd jobs as bricklaying. "In Vienna I became," he later wrote, "a convinced anti-Semite, a mortal enemy of Marxian philosophy, and a Pan-German." Serving with the Bavarian army on the Western Front in World War I, he was twice wounded and received the Iron Cross. During the postwar political chaos, he organized a small group of malcontents, later reorganized as the National Socialist German Workers' Party.

Hitler was a character familiar in every German *Bierstube.* Shrewd, arrogant, he held forth on every subject under the sun, from food to world politics, from music to military tactics. Pompous and omniscient, he refused to discuss his ideas, but instead issued dicta and ukases. He mistook his intuitions for scientific fact and believed he knew all the answers to the meaning of history. He lived in a curious dream world, dismissing as insane anyone who disagreed with his judgments and disconnected monologues. In *Mein Kampf,* written while Hitler was confined in the fortress of Landsberg after the beer-hall putsch of 1923, and which later became the Nazi Bible, Hitler paraphrased some of the world's worst literature, including Arthur de Gobineau's *Essay on the Inequality of Human Races,* Houston Stewart Chamberlain's *Foundations of the Nineteenth Century,* Alfred Rosenberg's *Myth of the Twentieth Century, The Protocols of the Elders of Zion,* and ill-digested interpretations of Nietzsche, Schopenhauer, Mackinder, Haushofer, Frederick the Great, and Carlyle. The British historian, H. R. Trevor-Roper, describes Hitler's mind as "a terrible phenomenon, imposing indeed in its granite harshness and yet infinitely squalid in its miscellaneous cumber—like some huge barbarian monolith, the expression of giant strength and savage genius, surrounded by a festering heap of refuse—old tins and dead vermin, ashes and eggshells and ordure—the intellectual *detritus* of centuries." This was the psychopathic personality fated to become Germany's dictator. "May God help the German people," Goethe had said once, "if a Napoleon appears amongst them."

Emergence of National Socialism. Adolf Hitler made political capital of Germany's misery. Within a comparatively short time he drew into the National Socialist party such discontented elements as disgruntled war veterans, poor students, ambitious monarchists, struggling shopkeepers, dissatisfied workers, frightened industrialists, anti-Semites, anti-Catholics, anti-liberals, anti-Socialists, anti-Communists, and unreconciled nationalists. A hypnotic orator, Hitler promised his followers the abrogation of the Treaty of Versailles, an end to the "war-guilt lie," the restriction of citizenship rights to those of "Aryan" racial origin, expulsion of aliens from Germany, the nationalization of industries, land reform, a highly centralized government, the restoration of German colonies, anti-Semitism, economic prosperity, and a mighty, invincible army. Nazi political strength gradually increased until in the Reichstag elections of July, 1932 the Hitler party received 230 seats, against 133 for the Social Democrats, and 97 for the Catholic

Centrists. When the Social Democrats and the Communists, irreconcilable opponents, refused to combine against the Nazi threat, they sealed the republic's doom. On January 30, 1933, President von Hindenburg appointed Hitler as Chancellor.

Once installed in office, Hitler set about .obliterating democracy and fashioning a totalitarian state. He ruthlessly destroyed all opposing political parties; dissolved the trade unions and confiscated their property and funds; abrogated all individual rights guaranteed by the Weimar constitution; and coördinated every phase of national life, including church, press, education, industry, and army. A shocked world witnessed a barbarous campaign "to protect German honor" against the Jews who numbered about one per cent of the population. Hitler himself assumed executive, legislative, and judicial powers, while passionately proclaiming the legality of all his actions. Abolishing all other political parties, he decreed that there was to be only one party in Germany, the National Socialist. In a sweeping program of centralization, he placed the federal, state, and local governments under his absolute authority. On June 30, 1934, in a barbaric blood-purge, he liquidated several hundred of his followers who had attempted to extend the revolution.

Coördination of Church. Hitler sought to subordinate religion to the State by throwing pastors and priests alike into concentration camps. He further tried to split Protestantism by organizing a German-Christian Church, which, as a new form of "positive Christianity," was to be subjected to State control. He violated a concordat with the Catholic Church, made in July, 1933, by which he had promised that Catholics would not be molested as long as they remained aloof from politics. In the meantime, he sought to win the German public to a neo-pagan movement, denying Christianity and re-creating the old Teutonic mythology. The churches did not submit as quietly as had German citizens. There were spirited, if unsuccessful, protests from all corners of the Third Reich.

Nazi Economy. The Nazi *Fuehrer* aimed to bring the national economy in line with his own principle of self-sufficiency. He solved the problem of unemployment by dismissing enemies of the State, decreeing compulsory military service, providing for extensive public works, and organizing labor camps. He obtained funds for the remilitarization of Germany by a system of forced loans from banks, industries, and insurance companies, and by suspending payments on foreign debts. In 1936 he launched a four-year plan to make the nation economically independent and self-sufficient. Without an adequate gold supply, Germany adopted a barter system to compete with other countries of the world for markets.

Nazi Culture. The Third Reich subordinated all cultural activities to Nazi ideology. Schools were transformed into agencies for propaganda, and women were returned to the kitchen. All cultural activities in the state were required to imbue citizens with the ideas of glorification of the Leader, fanatical worship for the Fatherland, intolerant racial prejudice, hatred for enemies of the Third Reich, blind obedience, and zest for war. Dr. Paul Joseph Goebbels, Hitler's Minister of Propaganda and Public Enlightenment, was assigned the task of coordinating all cultural activities. (*See Document No. 9.*)

Foreign Affairs. Hitler's foreign policy was to regain Germany's prestige as a world power, bring about the restoration of her colonies, promote Pan-Germanism ("One Reich, One People, One *Fuehrer*"), and revive the *Drang nach Osten*. To free Germany from what he called the shackles of Versailles, Hitler in March, 1935 announced the rearmament of Germany, reintroduced conscription, enlarged the army and navy, and launched a formidable air force. The next year German troops, in violation of the Locarno Treaties, marched into the Rhineland. Now emboldened, Hitler officially repudiated Article 231 (the war-guilt clause) of the Treaty of Versailles. On March 15, 1938, in order "to preserve Austria," he formally incorporated that state into the Third Reich. After signing the Munich Pact in September, 1938, Hitler announced that his territorial aims in Europe were satisfied. His invasion of Poland in 1939 brought on World War II.

Estimate of Nazism. The Nazi régime in power represented a descent into vulgarization and bestiality such as the world had seldom witnessed. How was it possible for a highly civilized people such as the Germans to allow themselves to be placed in this cunningly devised strait jacket? The complete mastery of Germany by the Nazis was due only in part to the ruthless suppression of all opposition. More important, it was the result of a national tradition of discipline and obedience, grounded into the Germans by a combination of Hegelian worship of the State, Prussian intransigence, and militarism.

The contention that Nazi extremism was a bolt out of the heavens, a "catastrophe" that was suddenly visited upon the German people, is inaccurate and untenable. German extremism did not occur in a vacuum; its roots lay deep in German history for a century and a half. Behind it was a pattern of thinking tempered by nationalism, romanticism, and historicism. The Germans who were shocked and amazed by the excesses of Hitlerism never understood that the political régime that had led them almost to national destruction was the logical outcome of a long and dangerous intellectual tradition. Despite its claims of historical novelty in seeking to combine the waves of nationalism and socialism, the Nazi movement in reality was stale and unoriginal. There was little new in Nazism other than the fanatical and ferocious methods used to implement its ideology.

German respect for power, *die Obrigkeit,* for the uniform, the title, and the office is not, as has so often been maintained, a trivial and unimportant stereotype, but, on the contrary, a characteristic deeply rooted in German history. The traditional German respect for authority from above resulted in an undiscriminating loyalty to the individual or party in power with no questions asked about the decency or indecency of the ruler or party. As a consequence of this slavish obedience and respect for authority, most Germans appeared to have only contempt for democracy as a way of life. The contention that the German national character is *congenitally* authoritarian is an invalid one, but there is much historical evidence to show that the environmentally produced traditions of authoritarianism, discipline, and servility led the Germans to accept dictatorship more willingly than other peoples. Added to this was a strong predilection for abstract ideas and cosmopolitan dreams. This preference for philosophic systems accompanied by a self-righteous rejection of the actual forces at work in the world resulted in a dangerous political immaturity.

Hitler, the supposedly omniscient *Fuehrer,* promised the German people a way out of their misery to the path of world power. Originally a bit skeptical about this strange Austrian, the Germans became more and more convinced of his infallibility as he delivered one crippling blow after another at the system of Versailles. As the unquestioned focal point of authority in Germany, he made sense to the Germans when he spoke of a Thousand-Year Reich. Politically illiterate Germans had little understanding of what was happening to them before the bar of humanity. It was necessary to invent a new name—genocide—for a stupendous crime against humanity—the slaughtering of millions of Jews by asphyxiation in gas ovens. The massacre of other millions, the devitalization of nations, the inhuman atrocities, all these horrors led the world to believe that the German nation had taken leave of its senses. There has been little to compare with it in the entire history of civilization. It took a worldwide coalition to bring the Germans down to earth and to smash their second bid for global domination.

17

SPAIN AND THE NEW, ENLARGED STATES OF CENTRAL EUROPE

Spain. The Spain of 1919 was still in a semi-feudal stage. Much of the land was owned by absentee landlords (grandees); industrial development was backward; political power was concentrated in the hands of the king; and three privileged classes—grandees, clergy, and *juntas,* or officers' councils—held social and economic power. There were strong movements for local autonomy in the provinces, especially in Catalonia, resulting mainly from the mountain barriers and poor transportation. These outbreaks were sternly suppressed. The nation was miserable and discontented. The government was weakened by its failure to quell an uprising in Spanish Morocco led by the chieftain, Abd-el-Krim. King Alfonso XIII, in desperation, installed General Primo de Rivera as dictator (1923-1930). After Alfonso's abdication in 1931, a Spanish Republic was established under Niceto Alcala Zamora, who separated Church and State, nationalized ecclesiastical property, confiscated the land of the grandees, granted Catalonia local autonomy, and introduced sweeping social and economic reforms. In the elections of February, 1936, the parties of the Left, including Republicans, Socialists, Communists, and Anarchists united in a Popular Front, won an overwhelming victory, and soon called for more land reform, nationalization of industries, and improvement of conditions for the peasants.

Supported by the propertied elements, the Fascist opposition, under command of General Francisco Franco, rebelled against the régime. The Spanish Civil War starting on July 18, 1936 was a bloody, fratricidal struggle marked by mass executions, air raids on the civilian population, and wanton destruction of property. What started out as a domestic struggle was soon transformed into a dress rehearsal for World War II, Italy and Germany siding with the rebels and Soviet Russia supporting the Loyalists. The bitter conflict came to an end on March 28, 1939 with the victory of Franco. Announcing himself as *El Caudillo* (The Leader), Franco ruthlessly liquidated all opposition and established a dictatorship in Spain.

Hungary. By the Treaty of Trianon, Hungary lost two-thirds of her land and three-fifths of her population. Shortly after the Armistice, Emperor Charles I, who was also King Charles IV of Hungary, abdicated, and a Hungarian liberal republic was established under the prompting of a wealthy nobleman, Count Michael Károlyi. In June, 1919, the republic was overthrown by Béla Kun, an officer in the Austro-Hungarian army who had been associated with Lenin and Trotsky in the Russian Revolution of November, 1917. The short-lived Hungarian Soviet Republic fell to the dictatorship of the Hungarian Whites under Admiral Horthy. Efforts to solve the desperate economic situation were fruitless. The most discontented of the Balkan Succession States, Hungary waged an unceasing agitation for revision of the peace settlement.

Other States. The Polish state had been abolished by the Three Partitions of 1772, 1793, and 1795, but Polish nationalism still existed. Poland was re-created at the Treaty of Versailles as a result of the efforts of three national heroes, Joseph Pilsudski, Roman Dmowski, and Ignace Paderewski, and the sympathetic attitude of President Wilson. The early history of the Polish Republic, founded in 1921, was marked by political quarrels, legislative chaos, and assassinations. Pilsudski came out of retirement in 1926, overthrew the government, and established a dictatorship. Polish domestic affairs were complicated by economic distress, the necessity for land reform, the treatment of such minorities as Jews, Ukrainians, and Germans and the persistent problems of the Polish Corridor, Danzig, and Vilna. Caught in the middle between rival great powers, Poland's foreign policy gravitated first to one side and then the other. Her continued existence as a sovereign state played a major rôle in precipitating World War II.

Doubled in size as a result of World War I, Rumania had a perplexing problem in handling her minorities of Transylvanian Magyars, Bessarabians, Ukrainians, Germans, Jews, and Bulgarians. Although she signed minority treaties, Rumania was accused of maltreatment of her minority groups. Attempts were made to solve the land problem by confiscating the nobility-owned land and distributing it among the peasants. The Magyar landowners in Transylvania, objecting strenuously, obtained the support of Hungary in their appeals to the League of Nations. Rumania's government remained unstable. King Carol set up a dictatorship in February, 1938.

Yugoslavia, the kingdom of Serbs, Croats, and Slovenes, came into existence in 1919 under the rule of King Peter I of Serbia. The new kingdom was split into two major warring factions: the Serbs, Greek Catholic in religion and Levantine in culture, comprising 45% of the population, and the Croatians, Roman Catholic and Westernized, forming 37% of the population. The political history of postwar Yugoslavia, like that of the Balkans in general, was a story of riots, assassinations, and civil war. In November, 1928, King Alexander I set up a dictatorship; he was assassinated six years later on October 9, 1934 while on a good-will tour of France. While she sought to maintain her independence by joining the Little Entente, Yugoslavia fell to German aggression in 1941.

After successfully resisting Communist infiltration, the Finns in 1919 established a republican government and joined the League of Nations the next year. The great problem of the Finns was to maintain their existence as a neighbor of Russia. Finland fought with the Third Reich against Russia in World War II.

Esthonia, Latvia, and Lithuania came into existence as Baltic Succession states after World War I. All three nations set up republican forms of government, united loosely by a common fear of Russia. In 1934 a Baltic Union was formed to frustrate Hitler's Germany. The states fell temporary victims to Hitler in World War II and later to Soviet Russia.

18

FUNDAMENTAL CAUSES OF WORLD WAR II

Underlying Issues. Bidding farewell to the Allied Armistice Commission in 1919, a German representative made this skeptical remark: "See you again in twenty years!" The accuracy of this prophecy is not as striking as the fact that it represented the thinking in a climate of opinion that seemed to make war inevitable. The period between 1919 and 1939, called appropriately The Long Armistice, saw an extension of all the motivating factors that had led to the outbreak of World War I. It became increasingly obvious that the blood-bath of 1914-1918 had brought neither peace, security, nor democracy, and that the European system was undergoing further social and moral disintegration. The same conditions, with some variation, that had led to the outbreak of World War I existed now in more aggravated form.

Economic Nationalism. The failure of the victorious democracies to achieve politico-economic stability and the effects of the world depression caused havoc and panic among the nations of the world. Three dissatisfied powers—Germany, Italy, and Japan—regarding themselves as have-not nations, complained vociferously that they had not been given a fair share of the world's raw materials, markets, and areas to invest their capital. The democracies, disunited and unprepared, sought to retain their economic dominance of the world. For a time they were willing to make concessions to the clamoring have-not nations in the hope that appeasement would avert war, but their efforts to maintain peace were fruitless when it became apparent that the Axis would not be satisfied with anything less than global domination. In a world in which all nations wanted a favorable balance of trade and economic self-sufficiency, each country resorted to economic warfare, including protective tariffs,

93

managed currencies, subsidized trade, and cutthroat competition. The next logical step seemed to be the battlefield.

International Anarchy. The failure of the League of Nations to establish a system of collective security led individual members to revert to the traditional method of forming diplomatic alliances and alignments. Nationalism, far from retreating, became even stronger. Even the friends of the League admitted that it was unable to assure security. Others, for varying reasons, denounced it. The Italo-American historian at Harvard, Gaetano Salvemini, expressed a widely held view regarding the League: "The history of the League of Nations between World War I and World War II was the history of the devices, ruses, deceptions, frauds, tricks, and trappings by which the very diplomats who were pledged to operate the Covenant of the League managed to circumvent and stultify it. They were its most effective foes, since they were undermining it from within, while nationalists, militarists, and Fascists were attacking it openly from without in all lands." The Nazis ridiculed the League as "a joint-stock company for the preservation of the booty won in the war."

Militarism. Still another failure of the League of Nations was its inability to achieve any real progress towards disarmament. After the breakdown of peace machinery, the nations of the world once again turned to an unchecked armament race. Each country, suspiciously eyeing the growing armed strength of its neighbors, feverishly strengthened its own military machine. The dictators saw rearmament as the means to power and glory; the democracies, overburdened with economic troubles, sought to stave off the expense of armaments until the last moment. In 1933, the last effective year of the League of Nations system, the world's armies numbered 7,000,000 men, its navies totaled 3,000,000 tons, its military planes numbered 14,000, and $4,000,-000,000 were spent on armaments. In 1938, the year of Munich, the figures skyrocketed to 10,000,000 men, 8,000,000 tons in the world's navies, some 50,000 military planes, and $17,000,000,000 in armament costs. The French army alone had 800,000 men, with a trained reserve of 5,500,000, in a total male population of 20,-000,000. Men were deathly afraid of war, but the fear of its outcome led them to prepare for it.

Clash of Ideologies.   A new challenge to the West arose in the global strategic goals and the tactical flexibility of Nazi Germany and Fascist Italy. "War is eternal. War is life." This was the philosophy, expressed in six words, of Adolf Hitler. "Fascism is not an article of export," Mussolini boasted. Pouring vituperation upon democracy and self-righteously chiding it for its failure to solve the economic dilemma, the dictators pointed to their own version of totalitarianism as the logical order of society in the new world. "We are riding," they said, "the wave of the future." To the democracies this was nothing but a renascence of ancient tyranny. It was becomingly clear that something more than the sweetness and light of Locarno was necessary to resolve the critical issues. Neither side was willing to accept the view of the other nor to compromise with it. The choice lay between appeasement or armed force. Soviet Russia, considering the democracies the lesser of two evils, fought with them against the Fascist threat but promptly entered into a cold war with the West after Mussolini and Hitler had disappeared from the scene.

Psychological Implications.   Added to the powerful economic and political factors making for war was an important psychological fact. The sentiment of nationalism, dominating every phase of human conduct preceding 1914, persisted afterwards in more aggravated form. Men of good-will hoped that the peoples of the world, disgusted with the periodic descents into barbarism, would become converts to a spirit of international conciliation. Yet, despite the efforts of Wilson and others, the peace settlements remade the map of the world along strictly national lines. What was lacking was a psychology regarding the common interests of mankind as something precious. The fatal flaw was that the educational process had not been successful in conditioning people to regard war as outmoded in a truly civilized society.

19

IMMEDIATE CAUSES OF WORLD WAR II

Germany's Bid for World Dominion. The problem of war-guilt for World War I has never been satisfactorily resolved. Today historians are inclined generally to absolve Germany of exclusive responsibility for the outbreak of the war of 1914. The blame for *starting* World War II rests solely and squarely on Germany. Admittedly, the general politico-economic and psychological climate of the world was such that war could be expected, but the continual aggressions of Nazi Germany in a bid for world domination provided the immediate sparks for the world conflagration. The very existence of Nazi Germany was a critical threat to world peace. It is clear from Hitler's writings and especially from secret reports captured during the war that Nazi Germany's immediate aim was to conquer Europe and her ultimate goal was global power. Obsessed with the idea that the superior German race was destined to rule mankind, Hitler was ready to smash his way to domination or ruin. "For the good of the German people," Hitler said in his *Secret Conversations,* "we must wish for a war every fifteen or twenty years. An army whose sole purpose is to preserve peace leads only to playing at soldiers —compare Sweden and Switzerland." At the same time, the Nazi leader was informing the world: "I am not crazy enough to want a war. The German people have but one wish—to be happy in their own way and to be left in peace."

Stages of Aggressive Strategy. Hitler's actions must be understood in the light of a series of aggressive steps taken by Japan, Italy, and Germany. The initial stage came with the Manchurian dispute of 1931, when Japan seized Manchuria and established the puppet state of Manchukuo. The failure of the League of Nations to solve this dispute and the withdrawal of Japan from the League in 1933 set a precedent for further aggression in defiance of world public opinion. Italy's invasion of Ethiopia in 1935 and her annexation of that country in 1936 were the next steps. The League failed to halt aggression by imposing sanctions. (*See Document No. 14.*) It lost additional prestige when Italy resigned in 1937. Italo-German coöperation with the insurgent Franco in the Spanish Civil War of 1936-1939 was another stride towards World War II. When the Japanese in 1937 opened hostilities with China to establish a New Order in Asia, the League once again was unable to halt the aggressor. While this continual flouting of the League went on, the French extended their security system by signing a Franco-Russian Mutual Assistance Pact on May 2, 1935. The Russians passed resolutions at the Seventh World Congress of the Communist International, meeting in Moscow in July, 1935, condemning Japanese imperialism in the Far East and Hitler's actions in the West. On November 25, 1936, Germany and Japan replied by concluding an Anti-Comintern Pact. Shortly before this, Germany and Italy laid the foundations for the Rome-Berlin Axis, an agreement transformed into a formal tripartite political and military treaty between Germany, Italy, and Japan on September 27, 1940 (Pact of Steel).

German Foreign Policy. Although the statesmen of the Weimar Republic bitterly criticized the Treaty of Versailles, they, nevertheless, adopted a program of reconciliation. They coöperated in the system of collective security, obtained several drastic reductions in reparations, accepted membership in the League of Nations, and effected evacuation of the Rhineland in 1930. This conciliatory attitude was abruptly reversed in 1933 with the accession of Hitler. Insisting that Germany had never been defeated in the battlefield in World War I, but that she had been stabbed in the back (*Dolchstoss*) by traitors at home (Jews and Social Democrats), the Nazi *Fuehrer* struck one crippling blow after another at the system of Versailles. On October 14, 1933, Germany resigned from the League. On July 25, 1934, Chancellor Dollfuss of Austria was assassinated by Austrian conspirators in collaboration with German Nazis. In 1935 Hitler repudiated the military and naval clauses of the Treaty of Versailles. In 1936 he remilitarized the Rhineland, and denounced international control of the Rhine, Elbe, Oder, and Danube rivers. On March 12-15, 1938, he occupied and annexed Austria. The defenders of the system of Versailles, paralyzed by fear into inaction, did not lift a hand to thwart the German dictator. Like a shrewd prizefighter, he danced and jabbed, seeking an opening to deliver the knockout punch.

Munich Pact (1938). The Nazi policy of aggression was masked by use of the liberal slogan of national self-determination. Hitler's tactics, added to the Italian conquest of Ethiopia and Japan's war against China, made it clear to the Western Allies that a general war was imminent, despite the *Fuehrer's* promises. (*See Document No. 15.*) Unprepared for a major conflict, England and France avoided war for the time being by signing the Munich Pact with Germany and Italy on September 29, 1938. The new democratic republic of Czechoslovakia was sold down the river and partially dismembered. The Sudetenland, scene of Nazi activity, was annexed to Germany. Soviet Russia, although not invited to Munich, offered to come to the assistance of Czechoslovakia, but her proposal was rejected by England and France. Neville Chamberlain, the British Prime Minister, returned to London from Munich, waving a piece of paper and assuring his people that he had brought "peace in our time." The betrayal of Czechoslovakia meant the end of collective security. After announcing, in March, 1939, that all his territorial demands in Europe had been gratified, Hitler invaded and annexed the whole of Czechoslovakia, with the exception of the Carpatho-Ukraine (given to Hungary) and seized Memel. It was finally clear that the policy of appeasing Hitler was fruitless and mistaken.

Prelude to War. The next month, in April, 1939, Italy occupied and annexed Albania. At long last aware of the danger, Britain hastened to rearm, while France gave Premier Daladier dictatorial powers to prepare for the expected conflict. The British guaranteed Poland (*see Document No. 16*), Greece, and Rumania against

German aggression; both Britain and France began ne-gotiations with the Soviet Union. Apparently, both the Western democracies and the Soviet Union were anxious to turn the weight of Axis aggression to the other side. In the midst of these negotiations, the Stalin-Hitler Pact was signed on August 23, 1939, despite the mutually hostile ideologies of the two dictators. Hitler believed that the agreement would remove the danger of having to fight a war on two fronts, while Stalin suspected that Britain and France were primarily concerned with get-ting Soviet Russia and Germany involved in a war in which both would bleed to death. Although Britain and France had warned Germany that there was a point be-yond which they could no longer tolerate German ag-gression, Hitler sent his armies crashing into Poland on September 1, 1939. Fifty hours later, on September 3, Britain declared war on Germany.

— 20 —

THE UNFOLDING OF
WORLD WAR II

Blitzkrieg in Poland. Using *Blitzkrieg* (lightning-war) tactics, the formidable German military machine struck at Poland with speed and fury. Coördinated aerial, tank, and infantry thrusts paralyzed the defenders. Holes were blasted in the Polish lines, as foot soldiers poured through to hold the conquered ground and mop up any remaining resistance. German bombers destroyed com-munications behind the Polish troops, thus preventing reinforcements, supplies, and ammunition from being brought forward and upsetting plans for reforming the armies. A horde of German secret police, spies, and fifth columnists descending on Poland disrupted her war effort and will to resist. She was disastrously defeated within a few weeks.

As the German army rushed eastward, the Red army, in accordance with the Hitler-Stalin Pact, marched westward. The two invaders promptly partitioned Poland between them, Soviet Russia occupying the eastern half populated by Ukrainians and White Russians, and Germany taking the western half, containing Danzig and the Polish Corridor. Having been denied entrance to the Baltic by the democracies, Soviet Russia, as the partner of Germany, now proceeded to annex Estonia, Latvia, and Lithuania. The Finns resisted courageously but were forced to relinquish strategic ports, naval bases, and airdromes to the U.S.S.R. What the British had denied Soviet Russia as the price of a military alliance against Germany, the Kremlin obtained with the consent of Hitler. The League condemned Soviet Russia and expelled her from membership. In June, 1940, the Russians occupied both Bessarabia and Northern Bukovina.

Aggression in the West. Thoroughly prepared and already placed on a war economy, the Germans now launched a peace campaign, believing somewhat naively that the Allies would accept their demands for a redistribution of colonies, reduction of armaments, and a guaranteed peace. Britain and France, thoroughly disgusted with appeasement and having no further reliance on Hitler's word, categorically declined. Hitler replied with a series of thrusts at his weak neighbors. First, Denmark was occupied in April, 1940; Norway, where a British expeditionary force was overwhelmed despite fierce resistance, was conquered by June; then Holland, Belgium, and Luxemburg capitulated to the Nazi war machine.

The armies of Germany and France faced one another in what was called satirically a *Sitzkrieg* (Sitdown War). The world waited for the contest between the irresistible force—the Nazi army—and the supposedly immovable object—the French Maginot Line. Suddenly, the Nazi armies struck at France, broke through the gateway at Sedan, outflanked the Maginot Line, drove the British forces from the Continent at Dunkirk, captured Paris, and forced France to sign an armistice on June 22, 1940. The conquering Hitler danced a jig of joy when news reached him of the fall of France. Occupying most of the country, the Nazis allowed the establishment of a friendly Vichy government in southern France, under leadership of the elderly Marshal Petain, hero of World War I. Disgruntled Frenchmen rallied around General Charles de Gaulle, who established a Free French headquarters in London.

Rôle of Italy. Italy remained neutral during the early months of the war, but observing that France was about to fall, Mussolini joined Hitler in June, 1940, to help administer the final blow. President Roosevelt sarcastically described this action as a stab-in-the-back. In December, 1940, the British forces in Libya and Ethiopia inflicted paralyzing blows on Mussolini's African empire. Envious of Hitler's successes, Mussolini, in the meantime, invaded Greece, where his armies were unexpectedly hurled back. In the next few months the Italian fleet was almost blasted out of the Mediterranean by the British navy. The master was now forced to genuflect to the pupil as Mussolini desperately called to Hitler for help.

Battle of Britain. Immediately upon outbreak of the war the British navy drove the German commercial and naval fleets from the seas and began an intensive blockade. The Germans sought to break it by an unrestricted submarine campaign. A traditionally slow starter, Britain managed to survive the initial blows. All the dominions, with the exception of Ireland, rallied to her cause. On his opening address to Parliament in May, 1940, Winston Churchill offered his countrymen nothing but "blood, toil, tears and sweat," and defined his policy as one "to wage war by sea, land, and air, with all our might and with all the strength that God can give us." (*See Document No. 17.*) On July 19, 1940, Hitler, flushed with victory on the continent, offered to give the British a last chance to surrender before their complete annihilation. "I am not the vanquished seeking favors," he said, "but the victor speaking in the name of reason." The British maintained a contemptuous silence. Hitler countered with an all-out attack by the *Luftwaffe* on English ports, airfields, industrial centers, and London. This was the Battle of Britain, the first great air battle in history and the turning point of the war. Thousands of civilians were killed and wounded as the Germans sought to demoralize and terrorize the population as a prelude to invasion. The small Royal Air Force held ("Never in the field of human conflict was so much owed by so many to so few" was Churchill's reaction). The mass attacks suddenly came to an end on May 10, 1941, when Rudolph Hess, Hitler's psychotic deputy *Fuehrer,* piloted a plane to Scotland and singlehandedly sought to end the war by convincing Churchill that the British were destined for complete destruction.

War in Africa. Italian troops, pressing across the Libyan border in 1940, established themselves about sixty miles inside Egypt. In December, British troops, in a surprise attack that carried them half-way across Libya, administered a crushing defeat on the Fascist forces. Only by enlisting German aid was Italy able to recover some of the Libyan territory she had lost. The Fascist dream of empire, however, was shattered by the British in East Africa. British command of the Mediterranean was maintained by smashing a large part of the French fleet at Oran and the Italian fleet at Taranto.

War in the Balkans. After the defeat of France, Germany turned eastward. Weakened by fifth columnists, "tourists," and saboteurs, Rumania succumbed to German pressure, and King Carol fled as Nazi troops poured in. In March, 1941, Bulgaria decided to join the Axis and permitted Nazi soldiers to enter her territory. Despite their own resistance and British aid, both Yugoslavia and Greece were overrun in April, 1941. A German parachute force occupied Crete, as most of the islands in the Aegean Sea fell to the Nazis. The revised German strategy apparently aimed at a thrust through the Balkans and an eastward drive across North Africa to the Suez Canal.

War in the Near East. After having successfully

resisted the German thrust at Suez from Libya, the British turned their attention to the task of removing Axis threats at their lifeline in the Near East. In a short campaign, the British ousted pro-Axis forces which had seized control of Iraq, the site of valuable oil fields. When the French Vichy government permitted Nazis to use Syria as a base, the British sent their own forces and Free French troops into the French mandate and forced it to ask for an armistice in early 1941. The British, now assuming full control over Syria, promised her independence after the war. The position of Turkey changed with the fortunes of war. Although they had an alliance with the British at the outbreak of the war, the Turks modified their attitude towards the Germans as the latter marched through the Balkans. Then, when Germany declared war on Russia and the British took the opportunity to strengthen their position in the Near East, Turkey found herself under pressure from both Britain and Russia for active support against the Nazis. In August, 1941, British and Russian forces occupied Iran which had refused to expel thousands of Nazi tourists in the country.

War at Sea.   At the beginning of the war, German submarines, long-range bombers, and sea raiders took a heavy toll of British merchant shipping. With the aid of fifty over-age destroyers, exchanged by the United States for air bases in British possessions in the Western Hemisphere, the British were able to strengthen their convoy system. On May 24, 1941, the new 35,000-ton German battleship *Bismarck* engaged the 42,500-ton British battle-cruiser *Hood* off Greenland, and sank the British ship after a five-minute engagement. Jubilantly announcing the end of British supremacy of the seas, the German High Command was appalled to learn within three days that the British navy had trailed the *Bismarck* and had sent her to the bottom. In the meantime, the British navy, in coöperation with its air arm, virtually demolished the Italian fleet at Taranto (November 11-12, 1940) and Matapan in the Ionian Sea (March 28, 1941). While the British lost an immense amount of tonnage as a result of submarine and air attacks, their navy managed to keep the sea lanes to England open. Shipping losses were critical, however; the problem of reducing sinkings became a crucial one of the war.

Situation in Spring, 1941. Germany in the spring of 1941 was in a strong position, having increased her size from 180,976 to 323,360 square miles, plus 290,000 more in occupied but unannexed lands, and her population from 65,000,000 to 106,000,000. Hitler in April, 1941 had at his disposal 40,000 airplanes, 180 submarines, 363,171 tons of surface navy, 214 infantry divisions, and 12 panzer (armored and mechanized) divisions. Against this powerful force were pitted the might of the British Commonwealth, a worldwide public opinion opposed to Nazi aggression, and the resources of the United States. Hitler's strength had mounted rapidly but so had that of his opponents. Formerly he had been able to divide his opponents and then annihilate them one by one, but now the Nazi *Fuehrer* faced a world united in distrust.

Invasion of Russia. In August, 1939, Germany and Soviet Russia signed a ten-year pact of non-aggression. Less than two years later, on June 22, 1941, Hitler sent his huge war machine crashing across the frontiers of the U.S.S.R., unleashing a furious *Blitzkrieg* on a 1,500-mile front extending from the Baltic Sea to the Black Sea, on land, at sea, and in the air. As a pretext for the invasion, Hitler accused the Kremlin of treachery, of threatening the German frontiers, and of carrying on anti-German and Communist propaganda. Thus, at the choice of the Nazi leader, the German people were burdened once more with a dreaded two-front war. Describing his assault as a crusade against Bolshevism, Hitler, in reality, wanted to obtain wheat, oil, and mineral supplies in sufficient quantities to enable Germany to defy the British blockade. The strategy was obvious: a *Blitzkrieg* against three primary objectives—Leningrad in the north, Moscow in the center, and Kiev in the south. Churchill promptly promised economic and technical assistance to the Russians, despite his aversion for communism. Italy and the Axis satellites, Rumania, Czechoslovakia, and Hungary allied themselves with Germany. Vichy France gave its approval to the attack and severed diplomatic relations with Moscow. Finland joined the battle; Sweden granted permission for Nazi troops to cross her territory; Turkey proclaimed her neutrality; and Japan adopted a policy of watchful waiting. When the Japanese occupied naval and air bases in French Indo-China, in agreement with the Vichy government, Britain, the United States, and the Netherlands Indies retaliated by freezing Japanese funds.

Recovering from initial surprise, the Russians astonished the world by their fierce and effective resistance. In the beginning, hundreds of thousands of Red troops surrendered to the Germans, but Hitler's policy of treating the vanquished as slaves stimulated a stubborn reaction. Stalin called for a scorched-earth policy. The Nazis paid dearly for every mile of advance into Russian territory. On July 12, 1941, Soviet Russia signed a mutual aid pact with Britain. The United States promised aid. With the Nazi lightning war slowed to a crawl on the Russian plains, Hitler explained to his people that he had miscalculated the strength of the Red forces. "We made a mistake about one thing: we did not know how gigantic the preparations of this opponent against Germany had been, and how tremendous had been the danger which aimed at the destruction not only of Germany but of Europe."

War Behind the Lines.   Hitler found it increasingly impossible to pacify the 140,000,000 non-Germanic European peoples who by this time had been subjugated by the Nazi war machine. The conquered peoples refused to stay conquered. Driven by dissatisfaction over food shortages and the excesses of the occupation forces, Czechs wrecked trains, blew up munitions dumps, and destroyed factories supplying the German armies; Dutchmen killed Nazi officers and soldiers and threw their bodies into canals; and Norwegians organized a campaign of sabotage. A union of hate welded Frenchmen, Belgians, Yugoslavs, Greeks, Bulgarians, Rumanians, and Hungarians into a powerful counter-force. The myth of Nazi invincibility was destroyed on the plains of Russia. German occupation authorities sought to stem the tide of rebellion by ordering scores of natives to be executed for every German soldier harmed, by condemning hundreds to death for high treason, and by executing hostages.

Rôle of the United States. From the beginning of the conflict in Europe the sympathy of the American public was with the Allied cause. Isolationist sentiment, strong at the beginning, evaporated when the Nazi aim of global power stood clearly revealed. (*See Document No. 18.*) Prior to the war, American neutrality legislation forbade the selling of war supplies to belligerent nations. In 1939 a new neutrality law was passed permitting the sale of war supplies on a cash-and-carry basis, while forbidding American vessels and nationals from traveling in combat zones, obviously designed to prevent such incidents as the *Lusitania* sinking during World War I. In September, 1940, the first peacetime draft law in the history of the United States provided for the registration of 17 million men. The Alien Registration Act of 1940 aimed to curb any possible fifth-column activity. In 1941, Congress passed the Lend-Lease Act, empowering the President to take any necessary steps to insure the shipment of vital materials to Britain. (*See Document No. 20.*) Measures were taken to defend the Western Hemisphere by patroling the Atlantic Ocean, while American forces occupied Greenland and Iceland. In August and September, 1941, the sinking of American-owned ships led to an order to the American navy to shoot on sight.

Atlantic Charter. On August 14, 1941, President Roosevelt and Prime Minister Churchill formulated plans for a new world based on an end to Nazi tyranny, disarmament of aggressors, and the fullest coöperation between all nations for social and economic welfare. The dramatic meeting was designed as a counterthrust to a possible new Hitler peace offensive, and, at the same time, stated the war aims of the Allies. The joint declaration of the Atlantic Charter announced eight peace aims: 1. no territorial aggrandizement for Britain or the United States; 2. self-determination as the basis for future national boundaries; 3. government by consent of the governed; 4. improved economic and social conditions; 5. higher labor standards, economic adjustment, and social security; 6. guarantee to secure the peace after the defeat of Hitler; 7. freedom of the seas; and 8. disarmament of aggressor nations and relief for peace-loving peoples of the crushing burden of armaments. (*See Document No. 19.*)

Far East Crisis. Since the invasion of Manchuria in September, 1931, Japanese militarists had consistently pushed an expansionist program. The outbreak of the European war in 1939 gave them further opportunity to pursue an even more aggressive policy. Japanese designs on the South Pacific, particularly on the Dutch East Indies, the principle source of America's rubber and tin, brought a sharp warning that any attempt to seize those islands would be regarded as a hostile act. Japan replied in September, 1940 by signing a military alliance with Germany and Italy. The United States then placed an embargo on the shipment of war materials to Japan and froze all Japanese credits in the United States. Japan's special envoy, Saburo Kurusu and her ambassador, Nomura, held prolonged conversations in Washington with President Roosevelt and Secretary of State Hull, with the professed purpose of negotiating a peaceful settlement. The United States asked Japan to halt her aggressions, withdraw from China, respect the open door policy, and break her tie with the Axis. The Japanese, insisting that they would not deviate from their immutable policy of setting up a Greater East Asia, demanded an immediate lifting of the economic blockade.

While these discussions were still in progress, Japan suddenly made a surprise air and sea attack on Pearl Harbor, the American naval base in Hawaii, on Sunday, December 7, 1941—"a date which will live in infamy" —followed by a formal declaration of war. The American public, appalled by Japanese treachery, at once submerged all differences and united to repel the attackers. On December 8, President Roosevelt asked for a declaration of war against Japan, voted by Congress immediately. On December 11, Japan's Axis partners declared war against the United States which met the challenge the same day.

THE GRAND ALLIANCE
AND VICTORY

The Great Coalition. With Japan's attack on the United States the war passed into a new, global phase. On January 2, 1942, after a series of inter-Allied conferences in Washington, an anti-aggressor block of twenty-six nations led by the United States, Great Britain, the Soviet Union, and China signed an agreement binding its signatories to fight the war through to victory and to make no separate peace. Subscribing to the principles of the Atlantic Charter, these nations affirmed their conviction that complete defeat of the enemy was essential to defend life, liberty, independence, and religious freedom. The Latin-American countries either declared war against the Axis, broke off diplomatic relations with the aggressors, or granted the United States access to their ports. A Conference of Foreign Ministers of the twenty-one Latin-American republics, meeting in Brazil in January, 1942, adopted sweeping sanctions against the Axis including the breaking of financial, commercial, and economic relations.

United States at War. The United States went on a full war footing immediately after the first bombs fell on Pearl Harbor. All key industries were ordered to go on a twenty-four-hour day and a seven-day week. In his annual message to Congress in January, 1942, President Roosevelt outlined an arms production program such as the world had never known: for the year 1942 it called for 60,000 planes, 45,000 tanks, 20,000 anti-aircraft guns, and 8,000,000 tons of shipping. A War Production Board was organized to coördinate this vast war procurement and production program. Government agencies moved to conserve supplies, a rationing system was introduced, critical war industries were subsidized, and an Office of Price Administration was established to check rising prices. The stupendous cost of the war program, estimated at almost fifty-nine billion dollars for the fiscal year beginning July 1, 1942, was financed by raising taxes to the highest level in American history. Industry and labor agreed that there would be no strikes nor lock-outs for the duration of hostilities and that all contro-versies would be settled by peaceful means. Selective Service was extended to enroll some 25,000,000 men in the war effort. Congress conferred on President Roose-velt full war authority. Volunteer workers were enrolled by the Office of Civilian Defense to protect civilian pop-ulations from the hazards of modern warfare.

Japanese Advances. The unexpectedness of the Japanese blow in the Pacific brought a serious setback to the United States. Severe losses were inflicted in Hawaii, but much of the damage was soon repaired and the losses replaced. The Japanese capture of such islands as Guam and Wake severed direct United States lines of communication to the Far East. The loss of Hong Kong further impaired Allied naval action. Gaining a foothold on Thailand, the Japanese launched an offensive down the Malay Peninsula toward Singapore. The ultimate objective of the Japanese was the Dutch East Indies, particularly Sumatra and Java, with their untold wealth in rubber, oil, tin, and other essentials for modern war. The Japanese aimed further to prevent the flow of sup-plies from America and to secure bases for a possible invasion of the Australian mainland. The long distances and the dispersal of Anglo-American navies over all the oceans, as well as initial Japanese air superiority in the Far East, made the dispatch of Allied aid a hazardous venture.

Turn of the Tide: 1942-1943. In late 1942 and 1943 great rivers of supplies began to be set in motion among the United Nations as they rapidly gained mas-tery of the sea lanes. Sensational results were achieved by wartime research including radar, rockets, penicillin, and atomic research. The great Japanese amphibious offensive in the Far East came to a halt on May 7-8, 1942 when one of its task forces was caught in the Coral Sea northeast of Australia and was severely battered by an Allied fleet. United States marines landed on Guadal-

canal in the Solomons on August 7, 1942. In the meantime, on April 18, 1942, the first air raid on a surprised
Tokyo was staged by Lt. Col. Doolittle's medium
bombers. On June 3-6, 1942, the Japanese suffered a
major naval defeat at Midway Island.

Though suffering terrible losses in the German invasion, the Red armies continued to offer stubborn resistance. The tide of German conquest had been stemmed
following the arrival of fresh troops from Siberia and
British and American equipment, as well as the good
fortune of a severe winter. Soviet forces wrested the
initiative in late November, 1941 as they began a
steadily advancing counter-offensive, hurling back the
Nazis along the entire 1750-mile front. Having failed
to destroy the Soviet armies, the Germans now attempted
to reach Voronezh in the north, Stalingrad on the Volga,
and Sevastopol in the south. The German Sixth Army
of some 300,000 men under Field Marshal Paulus reduced Stalingrad to rubble by November, 1942 but was
not successful in investing the city against heavy Russian counter-attacks. In January, 1943, Paulus and his
staff were captured and his army almost annihilated.
Hitler was now unable to isolate Moscow and Leningrad.

In the spring of 1942, General Rommel launched a
drive across Libya and into Egypt, where he was finally
stopped on July 1 by General Montgomery at El Ala-
mein, just 70 miles from Alexandria. The British counter-attack reached Tripoli, 1400 miles from its starting
point, at the end of January, 1943. In the meantime,
on November 8, 1942, three Anglo-American landings
were made at Casablanca, Oran, and Algiers. At Casablanca, on January 24, 1943, the Allies called for
unconditional surrender. (*See Document No. 21.*)
Pressed by Montgomery from the east and Eisenhower
from the west, the Axis made a last stand at Tunisia
where there was a general rout of the German and
Italian armies in April-May, 1943. The victory in North
Africa was followed shortly by the invasion of Sicily and
landings on the mainland of Italy. Against stubborn
German resistance, Anglo-American forces reached Na-
ples on October 1, 1943 and Rome on June 4, 1944. At
the same time, the Russians delivered sledge-hammer

blows at the Germans, securing the center of the long front, freeing Leningrad and Novgorod in the north during the winter of 1943, and driving the Germans from Odessa and the Crimean peninsula in the south in May, 1944. Meanwhile, scores of German cities were reduced to rubble by British night bombing and American high-altitude daylight attacks. In more than five years of bombing, Germany suffered a toll of 305,000 civilians dead and 780,000 wounded.

Invasion of France: D-Day. "Overlord" was the code name for what was to be the supreme event of the year 1944 and one of the most remarkable expeditions in military history—the Anglo-American amphibious landings on the Normandy beaches of France. The June, 1944 invasion was a stupendous logistical undertaking. It was necessary to train a million and a half men in Britain and to construct two enormous artificial harbors to be placed along the invasion beaches. The storming of Fortress Europe and the Atlantic Wall was made with complete initial surprise. The German system of defense in France was quickly smashed. By July, 1944, the flow of troops from the United States reached 150,000 a month, and shipments of material approximately 150,000 tons a month. Over a million Allied troops pushed the Germans steadily eastward, bypassing Paris and literally cutting the Germans to pieces in a *Blitzkrieg* unmatched by previous German drives in 1940. By September, 1944, six of General Eisenhower's armies were drawn up against Germany's western borders.

Drive into Germany, 1944-1945. In December, 1944, the Germans, under Marshal von Rundstedt, attempted a desperate counter-offensive in the Ardennes sector, held mainly by United States troops. This Battle of the Bulge, penetrating the American lines for about fifty miles, was finally stopped by December 25. In January, 1945, the Russians opened a major offensive through Poland directly towards Berlin. The next month eight armies of the Allies began moving across the Rhine. Soon the Germans were deprived of most of their industrial areas. Disorganized and demoralized by powerful blows from both east and west, the German forces rapidly disintegrated, as the Allies rushed across Germany with little opposition. The Allied and Russian armies met at Torgau on April 26, 1945, splitting Germany in two.

Death of Three Leaders. In April, 1945, within a period of eighteen days, death came to three top war leaders. One of the architects of victory, President Franklin D. Roosevelt, whose buoyant spirit had been strained to the breaking point, died suddenly on April 12, 1945, less than three months after his fourth inaugural, from the effects of a cerebral hemorrhage. The last words he wrote in a draft for a Jefferson Day address were a fitting epitaph to his own life: "The only limit to our realization of tomorrow will be our doubts of today. Let us move forward with strong and active faith." Roosevelt's death was reported in the American press on an "Army-Navy Casualty List." The nation mourned the passing of a courageous and vigorous president who had led it through a shattering economic crisis and the greatest war in its history.

Less than three weeks later, death came to the man who wanted to be Caesar and the man who wanted to be Napoleon. Benito Mussolini, egocentric demagogue with Calvinistic determination and Cromwellian confidence, was the first dictator to go. Wandering in northern Italy as a Nazi puppet ruler, he was captured near Lake Como by anti-Fascist Partisans, and, together with his mistress, Claretta Petacci, was executed on April 28, 1945. "Let me save my life," Mussolini begged his captors, "and I will give you an empire!" The bullet-ridden corpses were strung up by the heels in the Piazza Loreto, and then dumped like carrion on the public square where Fascism had begun its iife. An eyewitness reported "this finish to tyranny as horrible as ever visited on a tyrant"; citizens of Milan kicked the body and spat upon the man who had promised them world grandeur and had brought them the odor of beastliness and the odium of defeat.

Within two days Hitler followed Mussolini to the grave. On April 30, 1945, Hitler and his wife of a few hours, Eva Braun, died in a suicide pact in a besieged bunker under the Chancellery in Berlin, the Wagnerian death accompanied by crashes of Russian artillery. Here was a man who by ordinary standards would be judged insane, but it had taken the combined might of three great world powers to bring him and his lunatic structure to the ground.

The fighting ended in Italy on the day of Hitler's suicide. By May 4 more than a million Germans surrendered in the north, bringing the war in Holland and northern Germany to its conclusion. On May 7, Admiral Doenitz, who temporarily succeeded Hitler as *Fuehrer*, accepted the surrender, and all hostilities ceased at 12:01 on May 9. With this unconditional surrender, the war in Europe was over.

Pacific Offensive. The Japanese, with their supplies cut off by Allied submarines and naval aircraft, were now on the verge of defeat. The predicted revolt in Asia against European imperialism had not materialized, despite the fact that the Japanese war machine had swiftly collected some 500,000,000 people, a quarter of the world's population. In November, 1943, American troops captured the Gilbert Islands and in January, 1944 attacked the Marshall Islands. Kwajalein was taken on February 6 and the Marianas by June in a series of island hops. General Douglas MacArthur, who had promised that he would return to the Philippines, landed at Leyte on October 20. Japanese attempts to halt these landings were struck down. Operating from newly won bases in the Marianas, American airmen raided Japan. The highway of empire was now cut in two.

Despite these rapid Allied successes, President Truman, feeling that conquest of the Japanese mainland might be a long and costly process, ordered use of the atomic bomb. The first A-bomb was dropped on Hiroshima on August 6, 1945 with catastrophic results destroying three-fourths of the city and causing the deaths of 78,150 people. Two days later, according to he terms of the Yalta Agreement (February, 1945), Soviet Russia declared war on Japan and began a drive on the Manchurian frontier. A second A-bomb dropped on Nagasaki on August 9 convinced the Japanese that further resistance was useless. Accepting the Allied terms on August 14, the Japanese signed the surrender document in Tokyo Bay on board the U.S.S. *Missouri* on September 2, 1945. American occupation forces had already landed in Japan.

— 22 —

THE WORLD SINCE WORLD WAR II

Fundamental Changes. The greatest and most terrible war of all times produced four fundamental changes in the international situation:

1. The old European states system, which had received a shattering blow in World War I, was now almost completely destroyed. France had lost her role as a leading Continental power. Britain was no longer able to follow her policy of balance of power by adding her weight against the strongest Continental country.

2. The area of decisive global power shifted from its old European habitat to the United States and the Soviet Union, each of which became the possible nucleus of world hegemony.

3. The discovery of new weapons drastically altered the old concepts of military geography. The industrial nations of the West, particularly Britain, became increasingly vulnerable in the age of atomic weapons.

4. The vital force of nationalism was extended to Asia and Africa, where colonial peoples, demanding self-determination and an end to imperialism, upset the political and economic *status quo*.

Peace Negotiations. Before World War II ended in August, 1945, the diplomats of the Big Three—the United States, Great Britain, and Soviet Russia—had already laid a temporary groundwork for peace. Roosevelt, Churchill, and Stalin met at Teheran, November 28—December 1, 1943, where plans were made for concluding the war, and where it was agreed that a general international organization should be established at the earliest practicable date. At the Yalta Conference of the Big Three, held on February 4-11, 1945, it was agreed that the liberated peoples of Europe would create democratic institutions of their own choice and that they would have restored to them the sovereign rights and self-government of which they .had been forcibly deprived by the aggressor nations. This declaration was violated later by the Soviet Union in establishing satellite states in Eastern Europe. Furthermore, it was agreed at Yalta that defeated Germany was to be divided into occupation zones; Germany was to pay reparations; and Soviet Russia was to enter the war against Japan. At the final wartime conference, held at Potsdam, July 17—August 2, 1945, the Allies fixed the terms for defeated Germany: disarmament and demilitarization; dissolution of the National Socialist Party and its affiliates; elimination of militarism; democratization of Germany; trial of war criminals; and stiff reparations.

Cold War. Wartime unity quickly evaporated as Soviet Russia sought to expand her area of influence and as the United States and Britain, which had deferred to Stalin's wishes at Yalta and Potsdam, refused to recognize further expansion. During the first postwar year, the Kremlin rapidly consolidated its power in Eastern Europe and then withdrew behind an Iron Curtain stretching from Stettin to Trieste. Settlements for Germany, Austria, and Japan had to be postponed. The rift separating the Western Allies and the Soviet Union developed into what was called a cold war, in effect a continuation of world conflict. On the one side was the free world, on the other the Soviet Empire and its vassal states.

The cold war was fought on several fronts—political, economic, military, and propagandistic. On the political front, with the prospects of world collective security dimmed, the old system of power politics—checks and balances through alliances—was revived. Both West and East sought for German support by promising to aid German desires for unity. When the Kremlin sought to establish a permanent sphere of influence in Iran, the Security Council of the United Nations demanded and forced the withdrawal of Russian troops. The United States returned to full participation in European affairs with the promulgation of the Truman Doctrine on March 12, 1947, preventing Soviet penetration into Greece and Turkey. Militarily, the American stockpile of atomic bombs and advances in nuclear armament gave the West a temporary tactical advantage. When the United States proposed the establishment of an International Atomic Development Authority to supervise the commercial and scientific use of atomic energy through a system of licensing and control, the Soviet Union killed it in June, 1948, by veto in the United Nations. The Marshall Plan, announced on June 5, 1947, proposed the full coöperation of the United States with the European states in a continent-wide reconstruction program. Some twelve billion dollars of Marshall Plan funds helped West Europe to rebuild her shattered economy. The North Atlantic Treaty Organization was born in 1949 as a political and military alliance against the threat of Soviet expansion. On the propaganda front, both sides used every instrument of communication in the battle for the minds of men.

The cold war continued into the 1960's. Although Premier Khrushchev announced his famous principle of "peaceful coexistence," he did not renounce the ultimate triumph of communism, insisting that "we will bury you" and that "your grandchildren will live under socialism."

German and Austrian Treaties. The Council of Foreign Ministers, meeting in Paris in 1946, in Moscow in the spring of 1947, and in London in the winter of 1947, remained deadlocked on the issue of the German and Austrian peace treaties. The Soviet representatives, refusing to yield an inch or to compromise, denounced the Western Powers as warmongers. When the Western Powers gave West Germany a larger rôle in the European Recovery Program, the Russians replied on June 19, 1948 with a blockade of the Western sectors of Berlin. A hastily improvised Anglo-American airlift supplied the residents of Berlin with the essentials of life, a strategy that could be met only by risking war. The Kremlin lifted the blockade in May, 1949.

Japanese Settlement. The initial steps in demilitarizing and democratizing Japan had already been taken during the provisional occupation by American troops under General MacArthur. On September 4, 1951, six years after the end of the war, delegates of fifty-two nations assembled in San Francisco. The Soviet bloc attempted a filibuster by calling for a harsh treaty with Japan. Forty-eight nations and Japan signed the treaty, reëstablishing the latter as a sovereign nation. The peace pact reduced Japan to the boundaries of 1854, handed over the Kuriles and the southern half of Sakhalin Island to Soviet Russia according to the terms of the agreement at Yalta (*see Document No. 22*) gave the Bonins and the Ryukyu Islands to the United Nations under a trustee administration, and deprived Japan of Formosa and the former German islands—the Marianas, Marshalls, and Carolines. Japan lost her entire overseas empire. Provision was made for reparations by negotiation, but no specific restrictions were placed on Japanese rearmament. The Japanese monarchy was retained and provision was made for Japan's resumption of diplomatic relations with other nations. The Kremlin lodged a formal protest against the peace treaty.

United Nations. The League of Nations, the first organization in history dedicated to the maintenance of world peace by international coöperation, was virtually moribund by the time World War II began. But the idea of an international authority did not die with the League. At a series of conferences during the war, including the Atlantic Charter meeting (1941), the Moscow Conference (1943), Dumbarton Oaks (1944), Yalta, Mexico City, and San Francisco (1945), declarations and resolutions were formulated as the basis for a new world organization. The Charter of the United Nations, adopted at San Francisco on June 26, 1945, was the result of a compromise between the big and little nations.

The United Nations is a general world parliament, whose principles and purposes are an extension of those of the League of Nations. The original membership consisted of those fifty-two nations that had participated in the San Francisco conference. The Security Council consists of eleven members, five of whom (United Kingdom, the Republic of China, France, the United States, and the Soviet Union) are permanent. In all matters except procedural, the great powers have the right of veto, desired at San Francisco by both the United

States and the Soviet Union, a right that in practice strongly hampered the efficient functioning of the organization. The General Assembly, a kind of town meeting of the world, is composed of five representatives of each nation, each delegation casting a single vote. According to Article 10 of the Charter, the General Assembly "may discuss any questions or any matters within the scope of the present Charter or relating to the powers and functions of any organs provided for in the present Charter. . . ." The Security Council, hampered by differences among its members, lost some of its stature. The third organ of the United Nations, the Economic and Social Council, is designed to promote economic stability and general welfare among all peoples. The fourth organ, the International Court of Justice, adjudicates disputes among sovereign national states.

Major United Nations Actions. The first major United Nations case led to the withdrawal of Russian troops from Iran (1946). The Communist-led rebellion in Greece faded after United Nations intervention (1946). The General Assembly sent a commission to Korea to set up a free government (1947). United Nations efforts for atomic energy control were thwarted by Soviet-bloc opposition (1946-1948). The U.N. affected a truce in Indonesia (1948), which led eventually to Indonesian independence from the Netherlands (1949). A U.N. commission obtained a truce in the India-Pakistan quarrel over Kashmir (1949). The U.N. denounced the U.S.S.R. for "violation of the Charter in depriving Hungary of its liberty and independence" (1956). In response to a U.N. demand, Britain, France, and Israel ceased an attack on Egypt and the Suez Canal; the U.N. Emergency Force stationed in Egypt became the first uniformed peace-preserving unit in United Nations history (1956). The U.N. intervened in Lebanon to restore stability and facilitate withdrawal of U.S. and British troops (1958). To restore order in the chaotic Congo, the U.N. sent a police force with troops from 18 nations (1960). The United Nations Congo force completed its conquest of Katanga Province January 21, 1963, and remained there to maintain the peace.

Estimate of United Nations. The United Nations

was a new and somewhat streamlined continuation of the League of Nations, more powerful in some respects and weaker in others. The fact that the United States played a vitally important rôle in the formation and the activities of the new world organization made the United Nations inestimably stronger. The Charter of the League of Nations had been appended to the peace treaties at the conclusion of World War I, thereby tying it up with the real or imagined grievances associated with the settlements. The United Nations, on the other hand, was an independent organization. The desires of the smaller states were taken into consideration in both the planning and functioning of the United Nations. The most significant advance of the Charter of the United Nations over the League Covenant was the new Article 43, providing for an international police force to prevent aggression, a considerable improvement over Article 16 of the League Covenant concerned primarily with economic sanctions. The United Nations, however, is burdened with a cumbersome machinery for employing armed force against aggressors. The organization has been weakened greatly by Russian use of the veto power in the Security Council. (*See Document No. 25 for detailed list.*) Another blow to the U.N. was the death of Dag Hammarskjöld in an airplane accident in the Congo on September 17, 1961.

Despite criticism, the U.N. demonstrated its capacity for flexible adjustment to emergencies. Perhaps its main contribution has been the prevention of a direct clash between the U.S. and the U.S.S.R. By providing a forum for the discussion of grievances, the U.N. has prevented the two giants from colliding in a holocaust that would destroy civilization.

United States as a World Power. The United States emerged from World War II the richest and most powerful nation on earth. Within five years after 1945 it doubled its industrial output, tripled the amount of money circulating within its borders, and quadrupled its savings. Fears that the quick demobilization of its fighting machine would result in a wave of unemployment proved to be groundless. At the same time, the American economy was beset by rising prices, fear of inflation, and a rapidly increasing national debt. There was a greater concentration

of federal powers on the domestic scene; the Government
stepped into the field of social services, public education,
and many other areas of national life. In foreign policy
the traditional preference of Americans for isolation gave
way to an acceptance of the responsibilities shouldered
by a great global power. The threat of Russian expansion led to a decision to accept the fact that world responsibility of the United States had not ceased with the
victory of 1945. The United States committed itself to
the task of containing Soviet Russia and defending all
states in the world which were threatened by Communism. The Point-Four Program promised American help
for the free peoples of the world. (*See Document No.
23.*) America's entry into World War I had marked the
dawn of world leadership; she was now thrust by destiny
into a position of awesome power.

The Eisenhower administrations (1953-1961) denounced Soviet interpretations of war-time agreements,
and informed "captive" peoples behind the Iron Curtain
that they could depend on American aid. On January 5,
1957, the Eisenhower Doctrine warned the Communist powers that the U.S. would allow no further Communist conquests in the Middle East. In 1957 and again
in 1958 the U.S. sent the 6th Fleet to the eastern Mediterranean to meet crises in Jordan and Lebanon. In his
inaugural address on January 20, 1961, President John F.
Kennedy, calling for a "grand and global alliance" to
combat tyranny, poverty, disease, and war, served notice
that the U.S. was ready "to pay any price to assure
survival."

United States attitudes on many issues of foreign
policy began to stiffen. In April, 1961, Kennedy approved
a plan for the invasion of Cuba by an army of Cuban
exiles and refugees trained in Florida and Guatemala.
The plan ended in disaster, and the image of the U.S.
throughout Latin-America was impaired. Its prestige
was in large measure revived when, in October, 1962,
Kennedy instituted a naval blockade of Cuba to prevent
Russia from supplying "offensive" weapons to that
country. Khrushchev, not prepared to risk war far from
Russia, took alarm and promised to remove missiles and
bombers from Cuban soil.

The United States suffered a grievous blow on November 22, 1963, when President Kennedy, while on a visit to Dallas, Texas, was assassinated by a sniper. The entire world was shocked and saddened by this senseless deed, which struck down a brilliant young executive at the height of his career.

Postwar Britain. With very heavy war casualties, her cities bombed, and more than half of her 21,000,000 tons of merchant shipping destroyed, Great Britain emerged from the war utterly exhausted. The nation was once again in a serious economic plight, since she had no money to pay for imports. Foreign competitors had penetrated her overseas markets, British methods of production were obsolete, and the coal, cotton, and steel industries needed modernization. Although Churchill had led the British to victory, he was unable to convince the British people that he was their proper leader in peacetime. At the general election of July 5, 1945, the Labour Party won 393 seats against the Conservatives' 198, thus achieving a clear majority in a House of Commons with 640 members. The Labour Government proceeded to nationalize Britain's major industries, extended social services, and, instead of removing wartime controls, maintained them in a policy of austerity. The pound was devalued, thereby forcing the British consumer to pay more for his essential needs, but also stimulating foreign trade by reducing export prices. Loans from the United States helped in this program of reconstruction. The Conservatives won a close victory in the fall, 1951 elections, after six years of Labour rule. The Conservatives, retaining the welfare state of the Socialists, continued a program of drastic economies. On February 6, 1952, George VI died and was succeeded by his 25-year-old daughter, Elizabeth II.

After the voluntary resignation of Churchill in 1955, Sir Anthony Eden became Prime Minister. Eden resigned (January 9, 1957) following the Anglo-French-Israeli invasion of Egypt. Under Harold Macmillan there was a striking increase in prosperity. In Macmillan's words, "Most British people have never had it so good." The Welfare State, guaranteeing a livable minimum from cradle to grave, brought full employment. Since costs had to be met by increased exports, "Export or die" became the new British slogan. The Macmillan government tottered in 1963 when Conservative War Minister John Profumo was driven out of the cabinet in disgrace after a sex-espionage scandal involving noble names. In October, 1963, Macmillan, in hospital with an operation, resigned and was succeeded as Prime Minister by Sir Alec Douglas-Home.

British Commonwealth. The old decentralized British Commonwealth was maintained after the war with continued economic trade preference but loose political ties. Britain withdrew as a mandatory power from Palestine in 1948. She tried to consolidate her position in the Sudan by encouraging an independence movement there. Burma was granted complete independence in 1948, but it remained within the British sphere of influence. Singapore once more became Britain's major Far Eastern naval base; Hong Kong was returned to British control. The most striking change was the official British withdrawal from India in 1947 and the establishment of the two Dominions of the Union of India and Pakistan. King George VI dropped the title of Emperor of India and a native Indian became Governor-General. Mahatma Gandhi, who had done so much for India during his lifetime, was assassinated by a Hindu fanatic on January 30, 1948. The Irish Parliament, repealing the External Relations Act in November, 1948, broke its last ties with Britain. In 1948 Premier Smuts was defeated in South Africa, and was succeeded by Dr. Malan, a fervent advocate of *Apartheid,* or segregation of races.

The Suez Expedition of November, 1956, brought condemnation by the United Nations and the fall of Prime Minister Eden. The American alliance remained a cornerstone of British foreign policy, although there were differences of opinion, especially on the Suez attack (opposed by the United States) and on recognition of Communist China (favored by Britain).

From Fourth to Fifth French Republic. After liberation from the Nazis, the French people threw out the collaborationist Vichy government which had ruled them from June 16, 1940, to the Allied invasion of 1944. Marshal Pétain, who had collaborated with Nazi leaders, was imprisoned on the Ile d'Yeu, where he died on July 23, 1951. Pierre Laval, his right-hand man, was executed before a firing squad on October 14, 1945. The Provisional Government, headed by General de Gaulle, who had organized the Free French movement during the war, lasted only from October 21, 1945 to January 20, 1946. In September, 1946, a new constitution was promulgated for the Fourth French Republic, retaining the old form of government by bloc.

From January, 1945, to July, 1954, France had nineteen governments, of which none lasted for more than thirteen months and one for only four days. These frequent changes of government indicated that France was still plagued by the old political instability and indecisiveness. Contributing to the political dilemma was the large number of parties, each with different interests. The heavy Communist strength reflected dissatisfaction with economic conditions rather than support of the Soviet Union's foreign policy.

France was beset by a multitude of economic woes, including loss of foreign trade, inflation, flight of capital, national deficits, and inability of the government to collect taxes. The industrial system remained comparatively inefficient with much obsolete machinery and equipment. The treasury was depleted by the heavy cost of holding on to the French Empire, as well as the high price of rearmament. The political power of the Communists went up and down with this irregular pattern. The relative ineffectiveness of the decrepit French system of taxation added immeasurably to economic troubles. The tax burden fell mostly on industrial workers and consumers. Because tenants insisted upon rent fixed years ago, there was little impetus to construct new dwellings to meet the acute housing shortage.

In May, 1958, a coalition of nationalists and conservatives brought down the Fourth Republic. The newly established Fifth Republic, under the leadership of General Charles de Gaulle, was a "presidential democracy" with strong executive and balanced powers. Many of the old problems (inflation, taxes) remained, but the French economy improved greatly. In April, 1962, de Gaulle announced that the exhausting war in Algeria was at an end.

His "grand design" for an independent Europe under French leadership clashed with the will of his allies and provoked a crisis in the Atlantic alliance in 1964.

The Federal Republic of Germany. The Third Reich, which Hitler boasted would live for a thousand years, went down to disastrous defeat after an existence of only twelve years. The Germans paid a heavy price for their devotion to this monomaniacal Austrian—ten millions killed and wounded, many missing in action or captured, more than seven million homeless, the rest of the population stunned and bewildered, and the cities in ruins. Hardened troops of the Allied occupation forces were sickened by the scenes they saw in the concentration camps of Belsen, Dachau, Buchenwald, and Nordhausen. Twenty-two accused war criminals were tried at Nuremberg from November, 1945 to October, 1946, of whom twelve were sentenced to death, seven to varying terms of imprisonment, and three were acquitted.

Under the Potsdam Agreement, the victor powers divided Germany into four zones of control, American, British, Russian, and French, cutting across the old established state and provincial boundaries. Greater Berlin was split into four sectors, forming a fifth zone. The occupying authorities began to purge Germany of Nazis and Nazism and to destroy the foundations of the shaky structure built by Hitler. After 1947 the attempts to demilitarize, de-cartelize, and democratize Germany were weakened by increasing friction between the West and the Soviet Union.

In September, 1949, Dr. Theodor Heuss was elected first President of the Federal Republic of Germany. The new republic embraced slightly more than half the area of pre-war Germany but nearly three-quarters of its population. The capital was established at the old university city of Bonn, where a federal parliament functioned under a new constitution based upon that of the Weimar Republic. Great Britain, the United States, and France retained authority for the time being over remilitarization, reparations, de-cartelization, and foreign affairs. In 1951 Germany was invited to create a military force and to unite it with the armies of the West. On May 26, 1952, West Germany was indirectly integrated into the North

Atlantic Alliance by signing a peace contract with the Western powers which included her in the community of free nations as an equal partner.

The Federal Republic was heavily subsidized by its Western sponsors, particularly the United States. Under the conservative Chancellor, Konrad Adenauer, West Germany made a rapid economic recovery. German consumer goods began flowing in such quantities to the markets of the world that some countries, notably Britain, began to fear a price competition that they could not meet. The German automotive industry, starting with gutted factories and scattered labor forces, began to sell not just cars but complete assembly plants to Brazil, Australia, and Argentina. The real increase in the West German gross national product achieved a spectacular 8.8% in 1960 and 4% in 1962. Her industrial production in 1960 was 276 per cent above the level of 1936. She has sufficient surplus resources to give economic and technical aid to scores of underdeveloped nations, truly an economic miracle. Chancellor Adenauer, age 87, resigned on October 11, 1963, and was succeeded by Ludwig Erhard, the 66-year-old Economics Minister, architect of West Germany's incredible prosperity.

Even in its truncated condition, Germany became by 1964 again the foremost economic, military, and political factor on the European continent. As the kingpin of the Atlantic Alliance, she was wooed by both France and the United States. The Soviet Union and the nations of Eastern Europe feared the new power. American policy had to cope with the possibility of a new Rapallo, the eastward orientation of a united Germany.

East Germany. A few weeks after the formation of the Federal Republic, the Russians, who had ostentatiously avoided taking the first step in the splitting of Germany, formed the People's Republic in the East with Berlin as the capital city. Controlled by the Kremlin, East Germany was quickly converted into a Soviet satellite state. The East German Republic, containing 27% of Germany's population and 31% of its area, was ruled by the Communist Party under close Russian supervision. Non-Communist parties were permitted to have a nominal existence, but they were not allowed to oppose acts of the régime. A People's Police was set us as the possible nucleus of an actual army. Economic conditions sank to the level of Soviet Russia. Refugees by the thousands crossed the "green border" into West Germany. The unpopularity of the Communist régime among East Germans was demonstrated in a serious uprising on June 17, 1953, in East Berlin. This was the first open revolt of the century by the workers themselves against a government claiming it was based on the working masses. Economic programs, adopted in 1958 and continuing into the 1960's, called for a rise in industrial production.

The Soviet Union. In World War II the Soviet Union suffered heavier casualties than the other Allied nations combined—16,000,000 dead and more than a hundred billion dollars in property damage. After the war the Soviet government proposed successive five-year plans to promote economic recovery. The goal of the Fifth Five-Year Plan, announced in August, 1952, was "to mechanize mining and labor consuming operations, to automatize and intensify production processes, and considerably to extend and improve the utilization of the operating plants and to build new ones." The Sixth Five-Year Plan, integrated with corresponding blueprints for the satellite states, ran from 1956 through 1960. Politically, the Communist Party, reinforced by the secret police, continued its rigid supervision over the people. Every effort was used to maintain the dominant position of the state in political affairs. No concessions were made to political principles, but some deviation from the Marxian norm was permitted in the matters of religion and family life. The Russian Orthodox Church was reestablished, divorce was made more difficult, and steps were taken to encourage large families.

Every form of human activity was integrated in the Soviet Union to strengthen and perpetuate the Communist régime; art, education, literature, and labor were regimented as a means of maintaining the orthodox revolutionary spirit. In foreign affairs, the Soviet leaders dropped their spirit of compromise with the Allies—the friendly sentiment that had existed during the war—and reverted to the traditional attitude of distrust and suspicion of the capitalist nations.

Soviet Imperialism. For several decades the Soviet leaders had hurled accusations of imperialist exploitation against the Western nations. As soon as victory was achieved in World War II, Soviet Russia embarked upon a program of expansion that quickly dwarfed other imperialisms. The Kremlin operated on the theory that a great opportunity was offered by the weakening of capitalism. The war had destroyed the European balance of power under which no nation had been able permanently to dominate Europe. Since 1939 Soviet Russia has brought under domination nine previously independent European nations and parts of Austria and Germany. When the Polish republic was reconstituted after World War II, the U.S.S.R. retained almost 70,000 square miles of that country. Soviet armies occupied and incorporated the independent republics of Latvia, Lithuania, and Estonia, as well as the Petsamo region of Finland, adding some 6,000,000 population in the Baltic lands to the U.S.S.R. Additional acquisitions included Sub-Carpathian Ruthenia, Moldavia, most of Bessarabia, East Prussia, the Kurile Islands, and the southern half of Sakhalin (the latter two by the terms of the Yalta Agreement).

Attracted by the softening of frontiers, Soviet Russia began to establish a large area of influence in the Eastern European area. Czechoslovakia, Hungary, Rumania, and Bulgaria were penetrated by Soviet agents, subjected to united front governments, and then placed under the supreme dominance of the Kremlin as satellite states. In Yugoslavia, however, Marshal Josip Broz Tito was able not only to declare his country's independence but also to maintain it against the verbal attacks of the Cominform. Further Russian attempts to expand into Iran, Greece, Turkey, and Korea were discouraged by Western resistance. It became the task of the United States to contain Soviet Communist expansion wherever it appeared.

By mid-century, Soviet Russia had become the hub of a Communist wheel that encompassed more than one-third of the population of the earth. About one-fifth of the land area of the world is controlled by the U.S.S.R. in a Communist block extending over much of the Eurasian land mass. Soviet Russia alone possesses an extraordinarily formidable military power, with probably 175 divisions, 40,000 tanks, 20,000 planes, 300 submarines, and atomic weapons.

From Stalin to Khrushchev. On March 6, 1953, the world was startled by the following broadcast from Moscow: "The heart of the comrade and inspired continuer of Lenin's will, the wise leader and teacher of the Communist Party and the Soviet people, has stopped beating." Joseph Stalin, the Soviet dictator, had died on the previous day at the age of 73 after being in power 29 years. Any attempt to catch the elusive personality of Stalin is an exercise in futility. He has been described as a combination of Ivan the Terrible, Peter the Great, Genghis Khan, and Adolf Hitler. His utterly ruthless policies were responsible for the death of millions by forced collectivization; he sent other millions to enslavement in labor camps; he eliminated possible rivals by a duplicity almost unique in history.

In Soviet Russia, on the other hand, Stalin was honored as the glorious ruler who had transformed a backward nation into the second greatest industrial power on earth. Communists heaped saccharine adulation upon him, hanging his portrait not only in every museum, but in every room in every museum. "Without Stalin," said the editor of *Izvestia*, "no one can understand or write anything of interest."

Following a bitter struggle for power among the eleven members of the *Politburo*, the successor of the "Great Stalin" was Georgi Malenkov, the loser, L. P. Beria, now denounced as a traitor, executed, and his photograph and biography removed from all Soviet textbooks and encyclopedias.

After a military interlude, Nikita Khrushchev, First Secretary of the Communist Party's Central Committee, gradually pushed his way to supreme power. On February 25, 1956, addressing the Twentieth Congress of the Communist Party, he exploded a bombshell by detailing the "crimes of the Stalin era." Since then, Khrushchev's policy wavered between an ideological thaw and, following the Polish and Hungarian Revolutions, a "re-freeze." This balance between rigor and leniency continued into the 1960's. Nevertheless, there was a new relaxation of tension and terror. In foreign policy, Khrushchev called for coexistence with the capitalist world.

The most striking recent development in Soviet foreign policy was the gradual estrangement with Red China. According to Mao Tse-tung, enigmatic ruler of Soviet China, the Russians abandoned Marx and Lenin, while he, Mao, was the only new and noble architect of people' socialism. In retaliation, Moscow employed against China the richly vituperative vocabulary built up in excoriating Trotsky-ites, revisionists, and "Fascist dogs." To the Russians, Mao was a "foul liar" who was "trying to destroy the unity of the socialist camp." Soviet Russia was obviously fearful of an expanding China.

Post-Fascist Italy. Following the armistice with the Allies on September 3, 1943, Italy joined the war against Germany as a co-belligerent. Postwar Italy was left in a precarious position, burdened by heavy losses, the end of her empire in Africa, political chaos, and a shattered economy. On June 2, 1946, the Italians voted to abolish the monarchy and set up a republic. One of the main aims of the de Gaspari cabinet was to restrain the Communists, who had obtained almost one-fifth of the popular vote in both national and communal elections. Economic reconstruction was helped considerably by American assistance under the Marshall Plan. The central problem was to increase the productivity of both industry and agriculture in a country that had some 2,000,000 unemployed in a working population of 21,-000,000. Energetic efforts were made to close the gap between exports and imports. The Italian government established a cordial relationship with the Vatican.

Remarkable progress in vitalizing economic life led to a boom in the early 1960's—a rare occurrence in Italian history. The Christian Democrats maintained themselves in power, closing ranks with other democratic elements against threatening reactionary parties, the Monarchists and Neo-Fascists. The Italian Communist Party remained one of the strongest in Europe.

Small States of Western Europe. In 1947 Belgium, the Netherlands, and the Grand Duchy of Luxemburg united in the Benelux Customs Union for the purpose of maintaining joint tariffs on goods from other countries and of abolishing duties within the union itself. The Scandinavian countries, having escaped from the war with relatively little damage, rehabilitated their economies, but because of their delicate geographical position vis-à-vis Soviet Russia, they were unable to negotiate a common defense pact. Switzerland came out of the war with her traditional neutrality preserved and with the most stable currency on the continent. Portugal and Spain were among the least affected of European nations. The government at Lisbon was in form a democratic republic, but actually it was an authoritarian régime. Franco's Spain, strongly criticized in the West as Fascist in character, managed to consolidate its position in the postwar years. When the cold war between East and West became intensified, the democratic nations began to regard Spain as an unsinkable aircraft carrier in the struggle against Soviet expansion.

In late May, 1962, there were student riots in Portugal against the régime of Premier António Salazar, and in Spain there were walkouts in several industrial centers and student demonstrations against Franco. Typical of the problem of small states in Europe was the announcement in September, 1963, of a new law creating a formal language barrier across Belgium: Dutch the official tongue in the Flemish north, French in the Walloon-dominated south.

Israel. By 1939 the influx of Jewish settlers had raised the population of Palestine from 50,000 to 500,-000, a tenfold increase. The Arab population refused to be reconciled to the admission of Jewish immigrants, and the resultant feud stained the Holy Land with both Jewish and Arab blood. The issue was further complicated when the British restricted the entry of Jews by a quota system, just when the systematic Nazi persecution of the Jews in Europe made their desire for a national homeland more urgent than ever. On May 14, 1948, the British departed, leaving Jerusalem under the guardianship of the Red Cross, the entire Holy Land to war, and the United Nations Security Council with the problem of maintaining peace in Palestine. That same day witnessed the birth of Israel. Chaim Weizmann was elected President and Ben

Gurion was named Prime Minister. The new state, a parliamentary democracy, became the fifty-ninth member of the United Nations in May, 1949.

The establishment of Israel stimulated the revival of Arab nationalism in the Near East. The League of Arab States, including Syria, Egypt, Iraq, Lebanon, Saudi Arabia, Transjordan, and Yemen, had been defeated in the war with Palestine in 1947-1948. Wracked by dynastic and political differences, the Arabs, nevertheless, continued their opposition to Israel.

Gamal Abdel Nasser, Egypt's strong man, made it clear that he would seek to destroy Israel one day. The Israeli army, small but highly efficient, remained in a state of alert.

Decline of Western Imperialism. Western imperialism declined precipitously in the twentieth century. World War I, called an anti-imperialist war, put an end to Germany's ambitions by depriving her of a colonial empire. The victors divided among themselves the colonial inheritance of the vanquished, only to find the imperialist system wavering all over the world. True, the holding of colonies and the theory of mandates—both maintaining the rule of advanced nations over backward populations—persisted, but the whole system of political imperialism was in collapse. The colonial revolt reached flood tide in the years imediately after World War II. It was one of the most sudden transformations in the history of civilization.

Africa. The vast continent of Africa, three times the size of Europe and rich in natural resources, had been carved up by European conquerors in the nineteenth century. After World War II, African natives began a zealous struggle to free themselves. In Kenya, or British East Africa, the British went to war with the Mau Mau society, a secret anti-white organization that was determined to drive out all foreigners. There was increased tension between whites and blacks in the Union of South Africa. Throughout Africa, from Spanish Morocco in the north to the Union of South Africa, the natives demanded liberation from European control, though not necessarily from European civilization.

New, independent states with African leaders and parliaments based on European models appeared. Within a generation virtually all the former European colonies were transformed into self-governing states. Typical of the new independent countries was Ghana, which achieved its independence on March 6, 1957, as a new member of the British Commonwealth. Almost overnight Africans were called upon to vote, form political parties, and decide issues of national policy.

The Congo. Indicative of the new problems in Africa was the struggle in the newly independent Congo to bring order out of chaos. United Nations troops, amid tribal fighting, were able to form a central government at Léopoldville. The rich province of Katanga, led by President Moise Tshombe, refused to join the Congo nation and insisted on independence. There was bloody fighting between United Nations troops and Katanga warriors until the U.N. was able to stabilize the situation in 1963.

Asia in Ferment. Asia, a continent of ancient cultures and gigantic revolutions, houses a vast population of some 1,665 million persons, as contrasted with Europe (including U.S.S.R.), 641 million; South America, 206 million; North America, 199 million; Africa, 197 million; and Oceana, 16.4 million. The critical problem of overpopulation was compounded by the policy of excluding Asiatic immigrants from other sparsely settled areas of the world. The teeming and growing population of Asia was burdened by a primitive economy, poverty, pestilence, famine, and an unending struggle for an uncertain existence. Years of exploitation by colonial powers left their mark on the vast continent. For every altruistic missionary, doctor, or teacher who worked for the welfare of Asians there were many promoters whose one and only desire was to build up a fortune at the expense of the natives. Some of the great achievements of Western civilization were introduced into Asia, but with them there were indifference, hostility, and injustice.

World War II ended with most of Asia in chaos. By this time, however, the West had sown the seeds of freedom and nationalism in Asia. Admitting that their governments were inexperienced and their economies backward, the peoples of Asia nevertheless insisted upon becoming masters in their own houses. The era of great Western empires in Asia was brought to an end. Semi-autonomous or autonomous states emerged—India, Pakistan, Burma, Laos, Cambodia, Ceylon, Vietnam, Indonesia, and the Philippines. The United States gave the Philippines freedom on July 4, 1946. Pakistan and Ceylon changed their colonial status to self-rule as Dominions within the British Commonwealth; Burma was given self-rule and left the Commonwealth. Indonesia won its independence from the Dutch. This transition from colonial status to nationhood took place within the framework of a tremendous struggle between the Free World and the Communist bloc for strategic and economic dominance. Ancient cultures were reshaped in this great historical upheaval.

Communist China. In 1949 the Chinese Communists overthrew Chiang Kai-shek and established a People's Republic, with Peiping as its capital. For many years ragged forces under the leadership of Mao Tse-tung had waged war against the government of Nationalist China. With weapons supplied mainly from Soviet Russia, the Chinese Communists conquered the mainland. Chiang Kai-shek retreated to the nearby island of Formosa, slightly larger than the state of Maryland, where he claimed to speak for the people of China. The 11,000,000 people of Formosa and the small Nationalist army were heavily dependent upon United States aid. The People's Government of China remained a source of difficulty for the Western powers. The United States, regarding the recognition or appeasement of Communist China as a loss to the balance of power in the world, persistently refused to recognize the Peiping régime.

Korean War. On June 25, 1950, the Republic of Korea was invaded by armed forces of the People's Democratic Republic of Korea. The United Nations Security Council, in an emergency meeting, declared the invasion a breach of the peace. President Truman ordered General MacArthur to aid the South Koreans. The North Korean armies, with the initial advantage of surprise, overran South Korea within a few weeks. The United Nations counter-offensive drove them back to the 38th Parallel by October, 1950. When General MacArthur crossed the dividing line and pushed on to the Manchurian border, he was met by Chinese troops. Apparently, the war was being pursued beyond its minimum objective. The conflict continued in 1951 until the front became stabilized roughly along the 38th Parallel. The fighting went on for another year while truce negotiations disputed over details and technicalities. An uneasy truce was finally achieved by the end of 1952. The United States forces suffered casualties of 22,209 dead, 91,730 wounded, and 10,815 missing; the total Communist casualties were much higher. By the Korean War the West served notice on the Communist bloc that the era of appeasement and do-nothingism was coming to an end.

Atlantic Area. From 1939 to 1947 the balance of power in Europe shifted drastically as the Soviet Union annexed 200,000 square miles of European territory with some 24,000,000 inhabitants and exerted its pressure on additional countries. To save the rest of Europe from Communist domination, the Western nations began to consolidate. In the immediate postwar years the United Nations Relief and Rehabilitation Administration (U.N.R.R.A.) reached into some European areas. In 1947 Secretary of State Marshall proposed further support to the nations of Europe to prevent any additional disintegration. Under the European Recovery Program (E.R.P., Marshall Plan) billions of dollars were sent to the participating countries. On April 4, 1949, Britain, France, Belgium, the Netherlands, Luxemburg, Norway, Denmark, Iceland, Italy, Portugal, Canada, and the United States became the original dozen members of the North Atlantic Treaty Organization (N.A.T.O.), which agreed that an armed attack on any one or more of them in Europe or North America would be considered an attack against them all. In the meantime, there were other movements for European Union. The various plans were combined in May, 1948 in an International Committee of Movements for European Unity, which, in August, 1949, was organized into a Council of Europe. At long last an attempt had been made to establish a single parliament for all Europe.

Added to these efforts for political consolidation was a series of regional economic agreements. The Benelux

Customs Union, signed in 1947, was followed by the Brussels Pact of 1948, by which Great Britain, France, Belgium, Luxemburg, and the Netherlands agreed on a fifty-year treaty to collaborate in "economic, social, and cultural matters and for collective defense." In 1950 the French Minister for Foreign Affairs, Robert Schuman (died September 1963), proposed the Schuman Plan, which called for the union of French and German coal and steel industries under supranational control, as well as elimination of tariffs in the "core" nations of Western Europe—France, Italy, Western Germany, and the Low Countries ("Little Europe" or the "Inner Six" or the "Common Market.")

The pressure for integration—looser than union but tighter than alliance—continued. In 1956 the Inner Six pooled their resources of nuclear energy in "Euratom." In November, 1959, the seven nations of the European periphery—Britain, the three Scandinavian states, Switzerland, Austria, and Portugal—became the "Outer Seven," a counteragreement for the reduction of trade barriers.

President de Gaulle's proclaimed objective was to protect the continental economic and political community from what he saw as a threat of "domination" by the "Anglo-Saxons"—Britain and the United States. To this end, in January, 1963, France vetoed Britain's application for membership in the Common Market, voiding sixteeen months of painful negotiations. The British as well as the Americans were angered by de Gaulle's policy. Washington and London launched a major diplomatic effort to strengthen European opposition to de Gaulle.

Containment of Communism. These projects for military, political, and economic integration had two aims —to meet the challenge of the older system of power politics, separatism, and protectionism and to contain Communism. When the North Atlantic Treaty was signed in 1949, the military weakness of Europe was matched by its political uncertainty and its economic instability. Western Europe lay open to a Soviet army needing only marching orders to roll westward to the Atlantic Ocean. There were only fifteen under-strength army divisions from Oslo to Italy. European production was approximately at the 1938 level, and the problem of trade deficits was grave. By 1954 fourteen N.A.T.O. nations (Greece and Turkey were added to the original twelve) had pooled their military and economic strength in a unique working partnership. (*See Document No. 24.*) With 48 active divisions in Europe, a powerful force of jet aircraft, and 350 jet airfields, the N.A.T.O. powers possessed a defensive shield deemed sufficient to deter aggression. On October 3, 1954, nine nations (the U.S., Great Britain, Canada, France, West Germany, Italy, and the Benelux countries) signed a pact moving toward closer Western European unity (Act of London).

Indo-China. In the Far East the containment of communism hinged on a row of island defenses consisting of Japan, Formosa, the Philippines, Australia, and New Zealand. Indo-China, a treasure trove of raw materials, was the key to all Asia. In 1946 the French went to war with the Communist Vietminh forces led by Ho Chi Minh. The fall of Dienbienphu in May, 1954, was a great defeat for France and the Western world. Vietnam was divided into two parts, about equal in area, between Vietminh (north of a line along the 17th Parallel) and the French-sponsored government of Bao Dai. The states of Laos and Cambodia remained in non-Communist hands.

For a decade thereafter, the United States sustained a show of strength and patience to save the freedom of Vietnam. The alliance to defend South Vietnam against 30,000 guerrillas of the Communist Viet Cong summoned the presence of 14,000 United States troops and a cost of more than $1 million a day. The Viet Cong in 1964 began a terror campaign against United States personnel. The fate of the whole Indo-China peninsula depended on the United States and its desire to contain communism.

Areas of Friction. Vietnam was only one area of friction in a world plagued by trouble spots. In 1964 the cold war between Soviet Russia and the West continued. The Russians maintained their pressure on West Berlin. East Berlin was divided from West Berlin by a wall constructed by the Communists to prevent defections to the West. In the Middle East, tensions persisted between the Arabs and Jews. Africa was torn by factional disputes in the Congo, by colonialism in Angola. Latin America, burdened by economic instability, saw a Communist bridgehead created by Castro in Cuba and persistent danger of dictatorship elsewhere. The Far East was troubled by divisions in Korea, by militant Communist Chinese pressure on Formosa and India, by the Pakistan-India dispute over Kashmir, by Indonesia threatening war against Malaysia. Sore spots appeared all over the world in a kind of global political smallpox.

The Nuclear Race. On November 1, 1952, the United States unlocked the secret of the fusion process leading to the awesome hydrogen bomb. The first H-bomb explosion took place over Eniwetok, raising a force 250 times more powerful than the atom bomb that killed nearly 80,000 at Hiroshima. In August, 1953, the U.S.S.R. exploded a hydrogen device, an indication of the speed of Soviet nuclear progress. In November, 1958, both sides declared a test moratorium, since it was now clear that thermonuclear weapons could be manufactured cheaply and that any nation with a small supply of A-bombs could use them as trigger devices for thermonuclear bombs. In September, 1961, the Soviet Union ended the moratorium with extensive new test series. The United States, reacting with shock and anger, resumed testing in April, 1962. The position of the United States was that, in rejecting all means of true inspection, the Soviet Union was responsible for the new nuclear escalation.

In the summer of 1963 came a glimmer of hope when a nuclear test ban treaty was negotiated in Moscow. "Yesterday," said President Kennedy on July 26, 1963, "a shaft of light cut into the darkness." Although the ban called only for a halt to testing in the atmosphere, it was a reflection of Moscow's professed desire to have better relations with the West. (*See Document No. 25.*)

The alternative was an epitaph to civilization in flame and smoke. On a moral level, some called for an end of the idea of atomic retaliation. This point of view was expressed by Lewis Mumford: "Let us cease all further experiments with even more horrifying weapons of destruction, lest our own self-induced fears further upset our mental balance. . . . Let us deal with our own massive sins and errors . . . and have the courage to speak up . . . against the methods of barbarism to which we are now committed." Others held with equal vehemence that American atomic bomb superiority was the only deterrent to further Communist aggressions. It was an unescapable and agonizing debate.

Peace of War?   Some observers believe that the power in the hands of the two great antagonists of the world—the United States and the U.S.S.R.—is so great that neither side will dare to use thermonuclear weapons. Thus, peace rests on a foundation of mutual terror. Quincy Wright, a leading student of war, reminds us that nations do not necessarily stop fighting as their knowledge of more devastating weapons increases. The European powers alone have fought seventy-four wars in the first thirty years of the twentieth century. The "most enlightened century" has a record far worse than the previous 800 years. The issue of peace or war now appears not only to be urgent, but final.

— 23 —

THE MIND OF TWENTIETH-CENTURY MAN

Heritage of the Nineteenth Century.   The flowering of the Industrial Revolution brought tremendous industrial and scientific achievements but also a corresponding series of material inequalities. "The nineteenth century," says Crane Brinton, "was a time of extraordinary diversity of thought, an age of multiunanimity. Its extremes were great extremes, its tensions clearly marked—tradition against innovation, authority against liberty, faith in God against faith in the machine, loyalty to the nation against loyalty to humanity—the list could be very long indeed. Somehow the nineteenth century managed to keep these war-ring human aspirations, these basically conflicting ideals of the good life, in uneasy balance." The Victorian com-promise attempted to hold conflicting forces in check by attaining moderation in political democracy, nationalism, and capitalism.

The Twentieth Century. The twentieth century saw the greatest material achievements in the history of man-kind. But the kind of balance sought for in the Victorian compromise was shattered by two great wars and a great depression. The new intellectual and emotional restless-ness, as well as a new anxiety and insecurity, took the form of politico-economic experiments in communism, fascism, Nazism, and the welfare state, expressionism in the creative arts, and anti-intellectualism in thought. Con-flicts at every level in the nineteenth century were suc-ceeded by even greater tensions in the twentieth. Contem-porary man, like his predecessors, sought in his own way to find some sort of balance of his own, to solve the multiple problems of the machine age in an era of inse-curity.

Material Progress: Physics. The achievements of science and technology excelled by far the successes of preceding centuries. Most striking of all was the rapid and revolutionary development of physics. At the end of the nineteenth century the fundamentals of physical science were believed to be the Newtonian laws of motion and the principles of the conservation of mass and the conservation of energy. These basic hypotheses were modified or shattered by a series of important discoveries. The atomic theory of the composition of matter was abandoned in 1892, when Hendrik Anton Lorentz (1853-1928), a Dutch physicist, introduced the electron theory. In 1895 Wilhelm Konrad Roentgen (1845-1923), a Ger-man physicist, discovered X-rays and opened the field of radioactivity. In 1896 Antoine Henri Becquerel (1852-1908), a French engineer, discovered emanations from phosphorescent and fluorescent substances subsequently known as Becquerel rays. Pierre Curie (1859-1906), Marie Curie (1867-1934), Ernest Rutherford (1871-1937), and other scientists demonstrated that certain forms of matter, high in the table of elements, were disintegrating. In 1901 Max Planck (1858-1947), a German physicist, propounded his quantum theory, holding that energy was thrown from the atom in spurts rather than in a flow of uniform waves.

By the turn of the century it had become obvious that the atom was not a solid, hard, impenetrable mass but a tiny universe in itself, in which many of the previously accepted principles of physics failed to operate. Albert Einstein (1879-1955), a German-American theoretical physicist, published his special theory of relativity in 1905, projecting the idea that time and space were not absolute, as Newton had claimed, but were relative to the observer. Einstein's general theory of relativity (1917) and his unitary field theory (1931) extended his generalizations to include gravitational phenomena and electromagnetism. His work led directly to the construction of the atomic bomb in 1945. These discoveries made the scientist the magician and *enfant terrible* of modern society. "His modest guesses," in the words of Geoffrey Bruun, "abolish a plague or overturn a school of philosophy; his prescriptions bring life or death, poverty or plenty, to uncomprehending millions; his sibylline equations direct the course of destiny."

Technology. The twentieth century also marked a truly astonishing development of machinery and technology, revolutionizing not only transportation and communication but also the entire social order. Such servants of man as the locomotive, the steamship, the automobile, and the airplane were improved and developed into mechanical marvels. Engines, generators, and electrons became obedient slaves to the needs of man. The list is numerous: Diesel crude oil engines, motion pictures, radio, talking pictures, television, nautical gyro-compass, gyro-pilot, petroleum cracking process, televox, radar, cellophane, synthetic nitrates, nylon, precision instruments, and a host of other inventions and mechanisms. Twentieth-century man came to accept without wonder this array of mechanical marvels. The new technology was a force for both good and evil; its peacetime potentialities were enormous, but, unfortunately, it was utilized by dictators in their drives for world power and represented a force for evil when controlled by ambitious men.

Age of Super-Power. The twentieth-century industrial machine demanded ever larger quantities of nature's
energy. An amazing variety of power-hungry installations
consumed energy as fast as it was turned out. After World
War II, coal was dethroned as the king of fuels, largely
because of the inconvenience in obtaining it from the
ground as well as the high costs of transportation. The
coal industry was revolutionized, nevertheless, in much
the same way as the harvester changed farming. Additional oil was obtained by drilling through water to tap
off-shore supplies. The gas industry introduced big-bore
pipelines to transport its yield to metropolitan centers.
The energy of river waters, rushing to the seas, was harnessed by constructing giant tunnels and dams. Most
significant of all was the arrival of the age of nuclear
power. In the United States the Atomic Energy Commission prepared to use nuclear energy to run electric gen-
erating stations. Like coal-fueled power plants, the atomic
plants generate electricity by making steam in boilers,
using it to revolve turbines, which then turn the rotors of
electric generators. Experiments were made to run power
stations on solar radiation.

World of Electronics. Equally as promising was the
technological revolution in the wonder world of electronics. The transistor, a revolutionary substitute for the
glass vacuum tube, was invented, a tiny device that radi-
cally reduced the size and increased the effectiveness of
electronic equipment. Extraordinary computing machines
performed prodigious feats of mathematics. Work simpli-
fication devices were developed to produce vest-pocket
size radios, electronic cooking utensils, and machines for
cancer therapy. Microwave relay systems improved com-
munications.

The Race for Space. Still another aspect of the
rivalry between Communist and non-Communist worlds
was the headlong rush of brilliant scientists and engineers
on both sides to probe the universe. The world's best
brainpower was absorbed in this race for space. The
Russians sent the first two men into orbit—Major Yuri
Alekseyevitch Gagarin, who made one orbit around the
earth on April 12, 1961, and Major Gherman Titov, who
circled the globe 17½ times for 25 hours starting on

August 6, 1961. The first manned United States space shot was that of Navy Commander Alan B. Shepard, Jr., on May 5, 1961; the second was by Air Force Captain Virgil I. Grissom on July 21, 1961. Both these flights were suborbital. On February 20, 1962, Marine Colonel John H. Glenn, Jr., orbited the earth three times in a space capsule. The American launchings of men into orbit took place in the full glare of publicity. In June, 1963, the Russians launched Valentina Tereshkova when another cosmonaut, Major Valery Bykovsky, was already in orbit. The latter stayed up for four days, 23 hours and six minutes, while the first woman in space, Tereshkova, nicknamed "Seagull," logged 48 orbits—more than all the U.S. astronauts put together.

Both the United States and the U.S.S.R. instituted programs to put men on the moon within the next decade. Scientists began to question the belief that Earth was the only inhabited planet in the universe, and that mankind was the only intelligent race.

Medicine. One by one many of the most dreaded plagues of mankind were conquered; diseases that once threatened to decimate the population of the earth were rendered harmless. Asepsis and antisepsis, testing, and the cultivation of serums and vaccines cut the death-rate and led to the prolongation of human life. Among the recent contributions of medical science were hormone and vitamin therapies, improved anesthesia, synthesization of new drugs (insulin, penicillin, sulfanilamide and its derivatives), new understanding of bodily metabolism, public health developments, and increasing attention to mental ills. Modern medical research scientists, working collectively turned their attention to such unconquered diseases as cancer, high blood pressure, and multiple dystrophy. Typical of medical advances was the near-conquest of poliomyelitis by use of the killed-virus Salk vaccine, which was injected, and the live-virus Sabin vaccine, which was taken by mouth.

Philosophies of History. Despite his achievements in science, technology, and medicine, twentieth-century man remained troubled in mind and spirit. The eternal search for the meaning of history was now beset by a feeling of pessimism. Oswald Spengler (1880-1936) voiced a gloomy prediction in his *Decline of the West* (1918-1922), a deterministic morphology of history, warning that the urbanization and materialism of European society would soon lead to its decay. Arnold J. Toynbee (1899-   ), an English historian and educator, sought an explanation for the ills of the West in his *Study of History* (1934-1954), a comparative study of how earlier civilizations reacted in a rhythm of challenge-and-response. Piritrim Alexandrovich Sorokin (1889-   ), an American sociologist born in Russia, in his *Social and Cultural Dynamics* (1937-1941), presented an interpretation of history recognizing only a series of fluctuations between spiritual and secular eras that modern man could not hope to change. These and other challenging views raised more speculations than they resolved.

Philosophy: Positivism and Pragmatism. Philosophers, searching always for the eternal verities, saw the necessity for proposing a fusion of philosophy and science. Positivism, stemming from Auguste Comte (1798-1857) and oriented around natural science, strove for a unified view of the world of phenomena, both physical and human, through application of the methods of natural science. Systematized by Herbert Spencer (1820-1903) and supported by Charles Darwin (1809-1882), positivism as a philosophy continued into the twentieth century, keeping pace with the revolutionary scientific discoveries. A variation of this intense belief in the positive, the concrete, and the workable was pragmatism, born in the mind of William James (1842-1910) and extended by John Dewey (1859-1952). Pragmatism stressed the primacy of change, movement, and activity, the desirability of novelty, and belief in immediate experience. It urged use of a practical formula: "It's true if it works."

Sociology. The lag between material and social progress led to an energetic attempt to translate sociology into an exact and natural science. The Marxian theory of economic determinism, appearing in the mid-nineteenth century, became the inspiration of millions in the twentieth, while Marxists, orthodox and reformed, wrangled over its interpretation with religious fervor. Georges Sorel (1847-1922), a French engineer and social theorist, preached the dynamic activism of direct action and the general strike as the best way for the militant proletariat to seize control of society. Vilfredo Pareto (1848-1923), an Italian sociologist, put forward a vigorous argument for an objective social science, denuded of value judgments and resting on the experimental methods of the natural sciences.

Psychology: Behaviorism. Modern psychology developed a unitary purpose and a consistent formulation, despite the crisscrosses of opinion and the conflicts in definition and method. Psychologists no longer consider anatomical heredity to be the primary or exclusive determinant of personality. In 1913, John B. Watson (1878-1958) founded the behavioristic school of psychology, stressing environment as the more important determinant of human behavior. Ivan Petrovich Pavlov (1849-1936), a Russian psychologist trained in physiology, developed behaviorism by demonstrating that training (conditioning) could produce automatic responses in animals. For some social scientists this meant that the environment could be manipulated to give new organisms new responses. Behaviorism and reflexology were used by Communists to implement the theory of materialism. Other psychologists turned their attention to studies in motivation, mechanisms, and organization in an attempt to penetrate the psyche and see it whole.

Psychoanalysis. The search for the real inner self of man became a dominant passion among twentieth-century psychologists. The outstanding figure in this new quest was a Viennese physiologist and psychologist, Sigmund Freud (1856-1939), the father of psychoanalysis. Freud originally designated his theory as metapsychology, "a dynamic conception which reduces mental life to the interaction of reciprocally propelling and repelling forces." The great patriarch of psychoanalysis in its early days, Freud himself was no popularizer. His books, notably *The Interpretation of Dreams* (1900) and *Three Contributions to the Sexual Theory* (1905), were far too technical for public consumption. But he made a tremendous impact not only on scientists, but also on the general public.

Psychoanalysis, a specialized part of psychiatric practice, soon became a battlefield of factions. The first to break from Freud was his former pupil, Alfred Adler, who projected a new individual psychology, an interpretation of the interactions of the individual with society, emphasizing such dynamic units as feelings of inferiority and compensation for such inferiorities. The next schismatic was another Freudian pupil, Carl Gustav Jung, whose analytical psychology held that the flow of the libido is the entire system of psychic energy of which the sexual is only a part. Jung placed less stress upon sexual conflicts and substituted a theory of religious instincts for Freud's ideas about the unconscious sexual love of parents and their children.

Other important variations of Freud's theoretical and practical postulates include the work of Otto Rank (the birth of individuality); Karen Horney (abandonment of the artificial and cumbersome *libido* theory and search for an understanding of people in terms of social environment and the problems which it generates); Eric Fromm (logico-philosophical foundation for the explanation of man's nature and behavior); and Harry Stack Sullivan (interpersonal relations and emphasis upon the relationship of personality to the social order). All these deviant approaches of the post-Freudians admitted the value of Freud's researches into the subconscious mind and the part played by the subconscious impulses in human thought and conduct.

Psychoanalysis became the object of intense faith and the subject of bitter controversy. Since its subject matter was the submerged part of the human psyche, it was often attacked as a cult instead of a science. But to the medically well-informed, psychoanalysis, now more than a half-century old, has earned its place as a valued branch of the medical sciences.

Anti-Intellectualism. The twentieth-century trend of thinking as portrayed in philosophical systems, interpretations of history, sociology, psychology, and psychoanalysis revealed a deepening urge towards introspection. The tremendous material achievements of man in recent times were not matched by his ability to live with himself and with others. Crane Brinton called this passionate quest for man's inner self "anti-intellectualism," or the attempt to arrive rationally at a just appreciation of the actual rôles of rationality and non-rationality in human affairs. Fundamentally, the new approach is a protest against the overoptimism of the eighteenth-century Age of Reason, when it was believed that the aims of order, happiness, and individual freedom could and would be achieved. Anti-intellectualism held these same goals, but believed that they could be attained only imperfectly and very slowly on earth. The best way, it was said, is to work patiently at building up a true social science based on the long-tried methods of cumulative knowledge. Thus, while the term anti-intellectualism was seemingly a negative one, actually it presupposed that the new knowledge would be put to good use to promote the good working and the health of society.

Religion and the Collapse of Morals. The conflict between science and religion left a great split in the soul of twentieth-century man—material expansion and moral contraction, a schism potentially as dangerous as the atom bomb. Men failed to see, said Pascal, that "it is the heart that senses God, and not the reason." The fierce rivalries of nations, the horrors and carnage of two world wars, the fanaticism and brutality exhibited by human beings toward one another, all these caused contemporary man to wonder whether his moral and ethical life was in danger of collapsing. Some turned to religion, others became cynical, agnostic, or atheistic. State churches were disestablished in Soviet Russia, Hungary, Czechoslovakia, Mexico, and Turkey. Anti-clericalism and increasing secularization became the rule rather than the exception in a period described by religious leaders as beset with moral nihilism.

The New Education. The war of the spirit between the democracies and the dictatorships was reflected accurately in the basic field of education. The twentieth century saw a marked decline of illiteracy throughout the world but also differing attitudes as to how the young were to be trained. In an age of persisting national sovereignty, educational policy was subordinated to political ideals. The democratic nations struggled to preserve the integrity of the free mind and to permit individual development without indoctrination. Under dictatorships the educational system was thoroughly centralized, subordinated drastically to the aims of the state, and used to indoctrinate and regiment the young into obedient tools. Generally speaking, the new education followed the political philosophy prevalent in any country.

Literature: Era of Disillusionment. A significant picture of the development of world society can always be seen in the concurrent trends of literature. In an age of increasing materialism, with its concomitant anxieties, fears, and frustrations, the creative spirit was hampered by a confusing combination of social awareness, dissent, despair, and disillusionment. After the impact of both world wars there appeared literary trends characterized by a sentiment of moody resignation. The feelings of the lost generation after World War I were expressed by Thomas Stearns Eliot (1888-   ), whose poems showed a repugnance toward the industrial and materialistic civilization of his century. A similar disillusionment may be noted in the young writers following World War II, the new lost generation that turned to existentialism, an unsystematic conception of philosophy developed in France by Jean-Paul Sartre (1905-   ) ("We and things in general exist, and that is all there is to this absurd business of life").

When the bourgeois-dominated nineteenth century gave way to "the century of the common man," literary artists began to attack the middle-class pattern of society. Thomas Mann (1875-1955), German novelist, denounced the decadence of the bourgeois world and the sickness of an acquisitive society. John Galsworthy (1867-1933), British novelist, portrayed the slow disintegration of a British family gradually losing its bearings and sense of security. Henrik Ibsen (1828-1906), Norwegian dramatist, brilliantly satirized the artificiality and falsity of modern society, and urged social reform in a series of plays that were at first denounced as immoral. George Bernard Shaw (1856-1950), Irish dramatist and critic, satirically attacked the social conventions of his times and boldly pronounced himself a Socialist at a time when the word was anathema. Stefan Zweig (1881-1942), Henri Barbusse (1874-1935), Romain Rolland (1866-1944), and Bertrand Russell (1872-   ) attacked militarism and war as a reversion to barbarism and a disgrace to the human race.

The new psychology of Freud stimulated a school of writers to dissect the human soul and to probe into the mysteries of the human mind. Marcel Proust (1871-1922), French novelist, stripped the novel of its meaningless plots and sought for psychological penetration and introspective analysis. Henry James (1843-1916), American novelist, similarly turned to realistic psychological penetration and analysis. The Irishman, James Joyce (1882-1941), developed a stream of consciousness technique, through which he attempted to throw light upon the conflict between the worlds of the intellect and the emotions. Eugene O'Neill (1888-1953), American dramatist, wrote many grim and pessimistic studies of the people of his time, on occasion with mysticism and religious overtones. These writers and a host of others (Hemingway, Faulkner, Wolfe, Conrad, George Kaiser, Hardy, Aldous Huxley, Werfel, H. G. Wells, D. H. Lawrence, Sinclair Lewis, and others) portrayed a society in a mood of indecision, confused and bewildered, shifting in its human relations, frightened and insecure. Where eighteenth-century rationalists never doubted the eventual perfectibility of man, twentieth-century intellectuals saw a society in dilemma and human beings as aimless driftwood in a sea of troubles. It was a formidable century, they admitted, but it was burdened by increases in power and peril, by crippling anxieties and unsolved problems.

Fine Arts: Painting. Until the twentieth century the underlying motive in painting had been portrayal. The new esthetic formula of the artist matched the ferment and confusion of his times. Torn by conflicting ideas, artists, like intellectuals, agreed only in rejecting the older method of faithfully depicting nature and in searching for new modes of expression. Novel methods of painting introduced an intentional lack of correct depiction of forms, atmosphere, and color, as well as exaggerated means of awakening the emotions. Among the most gifted of these artists were Paul Cézanne (1839-1906), who broke away from the older techniques; Camille Pisarro (1831-1903), who introduced a deliberate distortion of form; Vincent Van Gogh (1853-1890), who used prodigious splashes of color in an almost barbaric display of intense emotion; and Paul Gaugin (1848-1903), who was inspired by the primitivism of the Pacific Islanders.

The search for expression went far in the work of Henri Matisse (1869-1954), who painted distorted pictures of primitive scenes but with a profusion of bold images and color-drenched canvases. Pablo Picasso (1881-   ) sought for meaning in geometrical designs. In Mexico there was a significant renaissance of mural painting, especially in the work of Diego Rivera (1886-1957) and José Clemente Orozco (1883-1949), both of whom combined Mexican Indian art with the symbolism of the machine age. Deviations of expressionism appeared in dadaism, stressing artistic freethinking rather than logic; constructionism, a mechanistic interpretation of the machine age; surrealism, a reaction against the precision of the realists; and cubism and futurism, emphasizing motion, mechanics, and energy. In the meantime, painting in Persia, Arabia, India, China, and Japan, more decorative than in the West, maintained its conventional approach.

Architecture. Modern architecture, with a wealth of materials from which to draw—new types of glass, reinforced concrete, steels, and alloys—was mainly utilitarian in design. Current architectural structures rely on simplicity of line but develop the simplicity to a point where it can suggest grandeur. The new railroad station in Florence, Italy, the *Bauhaus* in Dessau, Germany, and the Lever Brothers building in New York all used a streamlined effect with the utmost utilization of space and economy of area. Otto Wagner in Germany and Frank Lloyd Wright in the United States were the leaders of functionalism, a technique seeking to escape the old stylism and to develop an architecture suitable to the needs of modern life. Rockefeller Center, the Empire State Building, the George Washington Bridge, and an extensive series of apartment house buildings represented a fusion of mechanical needs and the age of power.

Music. The experimentalism of the scientific age brought about a new development of the harmonic side of music. Harmonic novelties, polytonality, fixed tonality, and dissonances were used to avoid the emotional elements in music and to concentrate more fully upon the physical impression produced by musical sounds. Much of the new music reflected the hardness and disillusionment of modern life, rejected old standards, and indulged in a constant, almost neurotic quest for new life. Russian composers, including Igor Stravinsky, Aram Khatchaturian, Dimitri Shostakovich, and Sergei Prokofieff, sought for new forms despite curbs on artistic expression in the Soviet Union. Arnold Schoenberg, Paul Hindemith, Béla Bartók, Jean Sibelius, Vaughn Williams, George Antheil, and others attempted new musical forms, although often some of them were responsive to the spirit of nationalism. In extreme cases, melody, polyphony, and structure were simply banished as completely worthless. In general, there was a lack of homogeneity in modernist schools of music, as composers sought among Asian and African peoples for inspiration and used elaborate experimentation in multiple themes and strange rhythms. The popularity of rock-and-roll music may be in part accounted for by the jaded and reckless spirit of youth searching for new modes of expression.

— 24 —

THE CONTEMPORARY WORLD

Promise of Progress.   It seemed at the opening of the twentieth century that a decent world society was in process of formation. The tremendous strides in science, industry, and communication had penetrated to all the continents of the earth. There was hope in the minds of men of good-will that, at long last, human beings would become aware of their common cultural heritage and would finally reject the cult of force as inappropriate to civilized society. War, the relic of barbarism, would be placed where it belonged—in the category of cannibalism. So it seemed to reasonable men.

Shattering Force of Nationalism.   In perspective it is clear now that this favorable prognosis was shattered by the continuing system of hostile sovereign national states. Some observers believe that the modern national state is scarcely the logical political unit for organizing the economy of an industrial age; others remain suspicious of any attempt to create a world order. The extension of political authority to continental or international spheres made it necessary for individual national states to rely upon their own power and that of military alliances. Rivalries between nations became more and more pronounced. Motivated by emotional interests surviving from the past, human beings tended to forget that all men are fundamentally alike as individuals. The necessities of integral nationalism made it imperative that other nations be defeated before one could live in peace. In theory the competition between states and coalitions could remain peaceful in the realm of politics and economics, but in practice war seemed to be preferable to national humiliation.

A World Society.   The transference of political sovereignty from national states to larger political units provided enormous problems for twentieth-century man. His history conditioned him to associate his material welfare and his emotional satisfactions with his national state. The bold experiment of the League of Nations after World War I disintegrated, and the nations of the world drifted back to nationalism. The tragedy of World War II drove home the idea to some observers that nationalism could not solve the difficulties of the world and that it was becoming increasingly necessary to achieve some workable form of world government. The difficulties of the United Nations, it is said, indicate that no suddent shift of sovereignty from the national state to world sovereignty can be made. Efforts to achieve a tentative regionalism, as a first step to a world society, have been made. There is some hope that the old notions of rigid sovereignty and segregation will be outgrown, and that integral nationalism will be rejected in favor of cultural nationalism with its emphasis upon tolerance and understanding of other peoples. Men of vision see the imperative necessity for submerging selfish national feelings in the interest of a common humanity.

The Fate of Man.   In contrast to the pessimism of Spengler and his fellow prophets of doom, other historians do their best to salvage what they can of the great democratic dream of the eighteenth-century Enlightenment. "Twentieth-century man," says Hans Kohn, has become less confident than his nineteenth-century ancestor was. He has witnessed the dark powers of history in his own experience. Things which seemed to belong to the past have reappeared: fanatical faith, infallible leaders, slavery and massacres, the uprooting of whole populations, ruthlessness and barbarism. But against all expectations of the totalitarians, by the middle of the twentieth century, Western civilization has proved its power of resistance against fanatic ideologies."

A similar refusal to be overwhelmed by cynicism may be noted in the penetrating ideas of an able University of Chicago historian, William H. McNeill. In his recent book, *Past and Future*, McNeill finds a basic pattern in world history through two psychological penchants among human beings—one towards intellectual innovation and the other towards habit, custom, and routine. There have been four critical innovations in human history, each accompanied by violent, revolutionary change—the pedestrian epoch, the equestrian epoch, the epoch of ocean shipping, and the epoch of mechanical transport. In the twentieth century we are in the midst of incredible changes in transport and communication. The United States and the Soviet Union are currently heads of transnational groups of states, each of which might eventually do for the whole world what Rome did for the Western world in the first century. McNeill hopes that this unifying power will be the United States, and that it will use its power to further democratic, liberal traditions stemming from the Enlightenment.

Let us hope, then, that despite the fears and insecurity of the present there may be a better future. It is possible that a new era of Western civilization, distinguished by close collaboration between Western Europe and North America, might emerge beyond the stage of xenophobic nationalism. The intense faith of Western man in liberty can survive the unpleasant troubles of the present. In the words of Winston Churchill: "It may well be that the lively sense of universal brotherhood and of the bright hopes of the future may stir in humanity those qualities which will enable it to survive the dread agencies which have fallen into its as yet untutored hands."

Part II—EXTRACTS FROM KEY DOCUMENTS

An understanding of twentieth-century history presupposes knowledge of a mass of documentary material. This section groups together for convenient reference selections from treaties, publications, speeches, and other material, that, in the opinion of the editor, throw light on recent historical developments. For a more comprehensive collection of readings, see the companion Anvil Book: *Fifty Major Documents of the Twentieth Century*.

— Document No. 1 —

THE AUSTRO-HUNGARIAN ULTIMATUM TO SERBIA, JULY 23, 1914 [1]

On July 23, 1914, the Austro-Hungarian Government sent a forty-eight-hour ultimatum to Serbia, which included the following pledge to permit Austrian officials to function on Serbian soil. Serbia refused to accept the ultimatum, deeming this demanded pledge a surrender of national sovereignty.

✦   ✦   ✦

. . . The Royal Serbian Government will furthermore pledge itself: . . .

5. To agree to the cooperation in Serbia of the organs of the Imperial and Royal Government in the suppression of the subversive movement directed against the integrity of the Monarchy.

[1] Max Montgelas and Walter Schückling, eds., *Outbreak of the World War: Documents Collected by Karl Kautsky* (Carnegie Endowment for International Peace, New York, 1924), Supplement 1, p. 603.

ORIGIN OF THE TERM, "A SCRAP OF PAPER," AUGUST 4, 1914[2]

After German troops had crossed the Belgian border on the morning of August 4, 1914, Sir E. Goschen, the British Ambassador in Berlin, called on Chancellor von Bethmann-Hollweg for a final interview. Goschen's report to Sir Edward Grey reveals the origin of the famous phrase, "a scrap of paper," which had an important effect on world public opinion.

✓   ✓   ✓

I found the Chancellor very agitated. His Excellency at once began a harangue, which lasted for about twenty minutes. He said that the step taken by His Majesty's Government was terrible to a degree; just for a word— "neutrality," a word which in war time had so often been disregarded—just for a scrap of paper Great Britain was going to make war on a kindred nation who desired nothing better than to be friends with her. All his efforts in that direction had been rendered useless by this last terrible step, and the policy to which, as I knew, he had devoted himself since his accession to office had tumbled down like a house of cards. What we had done was unthinkable; it was like striking a man from behind while he was fighting for his life against two assailants. He held Great Britain responsible for all the terrible events that might happen.

---

[2] *Collected Diplomatic Documents Relating to the Outbreak of the European War* (London, 1915), "British Diplomatic Correspondence," No. 160, p. 111.

— Document No. 3 —

SOURCE OF WILSON'S PHRASE, "TOO PROUD TO FIGHT," MAY 10, 1915[3]

Shortly after the beginning of World War I, the problem of military preparedness became a heated one in public debate in the United States. Preparedness was opposed by pacifist groups who insisted that the war did not involve vital U.S. interests. On May 10, 1915, President Wilson, in an address at Philadelphia welcoming newly naturalized American citizens, used a phrase, "too proud to fight," which infuriated his opponents, notably former President Theodore Roosevelt. Wilson later changed his advocacy of unarmed neutrality and his opposition to a large standing army.

The example of America must be a special example. The example of America must be the example not merely of peace because it will not fight, but of peace because peace is the healing and elevating influence of the world and strife is not. There is such a thing as a man being too proud to fight. There is such a thing as a nation being so right it does not need to convince others by force that it is right.

[3] *Address of the President of the United States at Convention Hall, Philadelphia, Pa., May 10, 1915* (Washington, 1915), p. 5.

— Document No. 4 —

ARTICLE 16 OF THE· COVENANT OF THE LEAGUE OF NATIONS, 1919[4]

The key article of the Covenant of the League of Nations was Article 16, calling for the application of economic sanctions (penalties) against any nation resorting to armed hostilities. Many observers attributed the weakness of the League to the fact that this clause lacked military teeth.

✓   ✓   ✓

ARTICLE 16. Should any Member of the League resort to war in disregard of its covenants under Articles 12, 13 or 15, it shall *ipso facto* be deemed to have committed an act of war against all other Members of the League, which hereby undertake immediately to subject it to the severance of all trade or financial relations, the prohibition of all intercourse between their nationals and the nationals of the covenant-breaking State, and the prevention of all financial, commercial or personal intercourse between the nationals of the covenant-breaking State and the nationals of any other State, whether a Member of the League or not.

It shall be the duty of the Council in such case to recommend to the several Governments concerned what effective military, naval or air force the Members of the League shall severally contribute to the armed forces to be used to protect the covenants of the League.

The Members of the League agree, further, that they will mutually support one another in the financial and economic measures which are taken under this Article, in order to minimize the loss and inconvenience resulting

⁴ From The Assembly of the League of Nations, *Bulletin No. 6,* September 1930, League of Nations Association.

from the above measures, and that they will mutually support one another in resisting any special measures aimed at one of their number by the covenant-breaking State, and that they will take the necessary steps to afford passage through their territory to the forces of any of the Members of the League which are co-operating to protect the covenants of the League.

Any Member of the League which has violated any covenant of the League may be declared to be no longer a Member of the League by a vote of the Council concurred in by Representatives of all the other Members of the League represented thereon. . . .

— Document No. 5 —

ARTICLE 231—THE WAR-GUILT CLAUSE OF THE TREATY OF VERSAILLES, 1919[5]

Article 231 (the war-guilt clause) of the Treaty of Versailles marked the first time in history that a provision of this kind was included in a peace treaty as a basis for reparations. Hitherto, the mere fact of victory had been deemed sufficient on the ground that to the victor belongs the spoils.

[5] From United States, 66th Congress, 1st Session, Senate Document No. 49, *Treaty of Peace with Germany* (Washington, 1919).

Article 231. The Allied and Associated Governments affirm and Germany accepts the responsibility of Germany and her allies for causing all the loss and damage to which the Allied and Associated Governments and their nationals have been subjected as a consequence of the war imposed upon them by the aggression of Germany and her allies.

— Document No. 6 —

ARTICLE 48 OF THE WEIMAR CONSTITUTION, AUGUST 11 1919[6]

The Weimar Constitution of the German Republic, initiated in 1919, is considered to be one of the most advanced democratic constitutions in history. However, the entire constitution could be invalidated in spirit by Article 48, which permitted the Reich President to suspend temporarily the Fundamental Rights guaranteed by the document.

[6] *Die Verfassung des Deutschen Reiches von 11. August, 1919* (Reclams Universal Bibliothek, No. 6051, Leipzig, 1930), pp. 17-18. The other articles mentioned in Article 48: Article 114 (freedom of the individual); Article 115 (freedom of residence); Article 117 (secrecy of postal, telegraph, and telephone communications); Article 118 (freedom of expression); Article 123 (freedom of assembly); Article 124 (freedom of organization); and 153 (personal property guarantee).

✓   ✓   ✓

ARTICLE 48. If a Land fails to fulfill the duties incumbent upon it according to the Constitution or the laws of the Reich, the Reich President can force it to do so with the help of the armed forces.

The Reich President may, if the public safety and order of the German Reich are considerably disturbed or endangered, take such measures as are necessary to restore public safety and order. If necessary, he may intervene with the help of the armed forces. For this purpose he may temporarily suspend, either partially or wholly, the Fundamental Rights established in Articles 114, 115, 117, 118, 123, 124, and 153.

The Reich President shall inform the Reichstag without delay of all measures taken under Paragraph 1 or Paragraph 2 of this Article. On demand by the Reichstag the measures shall be repealed. . . .

–– Document No. 7 ––

GIOVINEZZA, 1919[7]

Originally a World War I song, sung by black-shirted Italian infantrymen, *Giovinezza,* with several slight changes, was adopted at the Fascist Congress of 1919 at Milan as the official anthem of the Fascisti. Following are two stanzas.

✓   ✓   ✓

1.

Come, comrades in strong ranks,
Let us march toward the future.

[7] Verses by M. Manni, music by G. Blanc. Copyright 1923 by Mauro V. Cardilli. Translated by Dr. Vincent Luciani.

Let us be bold and proud phalanxes,
Ready to dare, ready to venture.
Let the ideal for which we fought so much triumph
    at last:
The national brotherhood
Of Italian civilization.

2.

Let not our people remain
Any longer craven or debased;
Let them reawaken to a new life
Of more powerful splendor.
Come, let us raise high the torch
To light us the way,
In toil and in peace
Let there be true freedom.

Refrain:

> Youth, youth
> Springtime of beauty,
> In "Fascism" is the salvation
> Of our liberty.

— Document No. 8 —

LENIN ON COMMUNIST
MORALITY[8]

That all notions of morality had to be harnessed to
class interests by Communists is indicated by these key
paragraphs from Lenin's writings.

[8] Nikolai Lenin, *Collected Works* (1923), XVII, pp. 142-45,
    321-23.

A Communist must be prepared to make every sacrifice and, if necessary, even resort to all sorts of schemes and stratagems, employ illegitimate methods, conceal the truth, in order to get into the trade unions, stay there, and conduct the revolutionary work within. . . .

We repudiate all such morality that is taken outside of human class concepts. We say that this is deception, a fraud, which clogs the brains of workers and peasants in the interest of the landlords and capitalists. . . . We say: "Morality is that which serves to destroy the old exploiting society and to unite all the toilers around the proletariat, which is creating a new Communist society."

— Document No. 9 —

THE *HORST WESSEL SONG*[9]

The Horst Wessel Song, the Nazi anthem, was written by a young street-fighter, who was made a national hero after his violent death.

1.

Hold high the banner! Close the hard ranks serried!
S.A. marches on with sturdy stride.
Comrades, by Red Front and Reaction killed, are buried,
But march with us in image at our side.

2.

Gang way! Gang way! now for the Brown battalions!
For the Storm Trooper clear roads o'er the land!

[9] Translated by the editor.

The Swastika gives hope to our entranced millions,
The day for freedom and for bread's at hand.

3.

The trumpet blows its shrill and final blast!
Prepared for war and battle here we stand.
Soon Hitler's banners will wave unchecked at last,
The end of German slav'ry in our land!

— Document No. 10 —

DEFINITION OF AN AGGRESSOR: ARTICLE 10 OF THE GENEVA PROTOCOL, OCTOBER 2, 1924 [10]

After 1919 the postwar efforts to achieve security were hampered by the lack of a satisfactory definition of an aggressor. The Geneva Protocol for the Pacific Settlement of International Disputes, adopted by the Assembly on October 2, 1924, was the first document that gave promise of preventing future wars by clearly defining the aggressor. The Protocol, opposed by Great Britain because it meant global commitments, was never ratified.

✓   ✓   ✓

ARTICLE 10. Every State which resorts to war in violation of the undertakings contained in the Covenant or the present Protocol is an aggressor. Violation of

[10] League of Nations, *Official Journal,* Supplement No. 23 (Geneva, 1924), p. 500.

the rules laid down for a demilitarised zone shall be held equivalent to resort to war.

In the event of hostilities having broken out, any State shall be presumed to be an aggressor, unless a decision of the Council, which must be taken unanimously, shall otherwise declare:

1. If it has refused to submit the dispute to the procedure of pacific settlement provided by Articles 13 and 15 of the Covenant as amplified by the present Protocol, or to comply with a judicial sentence or arbitral award or with a unanimous recommendation of the Council, or has disregarded a unanimous report of the Council, a judicial sentence of an arbitral award recognizing that the dispute between it and the other belligerent State arises out of a matter which by international law is solely within the domestic jurisdiction of the latter State; nevertheless, in the last case the State shall only be presumed to be an aggressor if it has not previously submitted the question to the Council or the Assembly, in accordance with Article 11 of the Covenant.

2. If it has violated provisional measures enjoined by the Council for the period while the proceedings are in progress as contemplated by Article 7 of the present Protocol.

Apart from the cases dealt with in paragraphs 1 and 2 of the present Article, if the Council does not at once succeed in determining the aggressor, it shall be bound to enjoin upon the belligerents an armistice, and shall fix the terms, acting, if need be, by a two-thirds majority and shall supervise its execution.

Any belligerent which has refused to accept the armistice or has violated its terms shall be deemed an aggressor.

The Council shall call upon the signatory States to apply forthwith against the aggressor the sanctions provided by Article 11 of the present Protocol, and any signatory State thus called upon shall thereupon be entitled to exercise the rights of a belligerent.

ARTICLE 21—THE ESCALATOR CLAUSE OF THE LONDON NAVAL TREATY, 1930[11]

The London Naval Conference of 1930 sought not so much to reduce naval armaments as limit them. The continuing suspicions of the signatories were betrayed by including the following "escalator clause," permitting each power to exceed the tonnage limits if in its opinion new construction by an non-signatory power threatened its own security.

↑   ↑   ↑

ARTICLE 21. If, during the term of the present Treaty, the requirements of the national security of any High Contracting Party in respect of vessels of war limited by Part III of the present Treaty are, in the opinion of that Party, materially affected by new construction of any other Power than those who have joined in Part III of this Treaty, that High Contracting Party will notify the other Parties to Part III as to the increases required to be made in its own tonnages within one or more of the categories of such vessels of war, specifying particularly the proposed increases and the reasons therefor, and shall be entitled to make such increases. Thereupon the other Parties to Part III of this Treaty shall be entitled to make a proportionate increase in the category or categories specified; and the said other Parties shall promptly advise with each other through diplomatic channels as to the situation thus presented.

---

[11] For the complete text see League of Nations, *Treaty Series 1931*, CXII, pp. 66-91.

MUSSOLINI'S DEFINITION OF FASCISM, 1931 [12]

Mussolini's conception of fascism was expressed in an article in the *Italian Encyclopedia,* from which the following is extracted.

✓   ✓   ✓

Fascism is a religious conception in which man is seen in his immanent relationship with a superior law and with an objective Will that transcends the particular individual and raises him to conscious membership of a spiritual society. . . . Whoever has seen in the religious politics of the Fascist régime nothing but mere opportunism has not understood that Fascism besides being a system of government is also, and above all, a system of thought. . . . Fascism is opposed to all the individualistic abstractions of a materialistic nature like those of the eighteenth century; and it is opposed to all Jacobin utopias and innovations. . . . Against individualism, the Fascist conception is for the State; and it is for the individual in so far as he coincides with the State, which is the conscience and universal will of man in his historical existence. . . . Liberalism denied the State in the interests of the particular individual; Fascism reaffirms the State as the true reality of the individual.

[12] Benito Mussolini, *The Doctrine of Fascism, Fundamental Ideas,* paragraphs 5, 6, 7, *Italian Encyclopedia* (1931).

— Document No. 13 —

FRANKLIN D. ROOSEVELT'S "FEAR" SPEECH, MARCH 4, 1933[13]

Economic conditions reached gravely critical proportions in the United States in early 1933. The unemployed numbered 16,000,000, two-thirds of the factories were idle, business was stagnating, and breadlines were common. In his inaugural address, President Franklin D. Roosevelt affirmed that "the only thing we have to fear is fear itself," a sentence that launched the era of New Deal reform.

✔   ✔   ✔

President Hoover, Mr. Chief Justice, my friends:

This is a day of national consecration and I am certain that on this day my fellow-Americans expect that on my induction to the Presidency I will address them with a candor and a decision which the present situation of our people impels.

This is pre-eminently the time to speak the truth, the whole truth, frankly and boldly. Nor need we shrink from honestly facing conditions in our country today. This great nation will endure as it has endured, will revive, and will prosper.

So first of all let me assert my firm belief that the only thing we have to fear is fear itself—nameless, unreasoning, unjustified terror which paralyzes needed efforts to convert retreat into advance.

[13] *The New York Times,* March 5, 1933.

— Document No. 14 —

HAILE SELASSIE'S WARNING TO THE LEAGUE OF NATIONS, JUNE 30, 1936[14]

After the annexation of his country by Fascist Italy, Haile Selassie I, Emperor of Ethiopia, made this prophetic speech at Geneva on June 30, 1936. He stood patiently at the rostrum before the Assembly of the League of Nations, while his efforts to speak were drowned out by shouting pro-Mussolini newsmen. The League rejected his plea that sanctions be continued, and thereby opened the way to the era of appeasement.

✓　　　　✓　　　　✓

I, Haile Selassie, Emperor of Ethiopia, am here today to claim that justice which is due to my people, and the assistance promised it eight months ago, when fifty nations asserted that aggression had been committed. . . .

It is my duty to inform the governments of the deadly peril which threatens them. . . . It is a question of trust in international treaties and of the value of promises to small states that their integrity shall be respected. In a word, it is international morality that is at stake. . . .

Apart from the Kingdom of God, there is not on this earth any nation that is higher than any other. . . . God and history will remember your judgment.

[14] Adapted from *The New York Times,* July, 1, 1936.

HITLER'S "LAST TERRITORIAL CLAIM" IN EUROPE, SEPTEMBER 26, 1938[15]

On September 26, 1938, three days before the conference at Munich, Hitler delivered a speech at the Sportpalast, in Berlin, assuring Chamberlain that, if the Sudeten problem were solved, Germany would have no more territorial problems in Europe. The world was led to believe that the *Fuehrer's* ambitions were about to be fulfilled.

✓ ✓ ✓

We now come to the last problem which has to be solved and will be solved.

It is the last territorial demand I have to make in Europe. In 1919, 3,500,000 Germans were torn away from their compatriots by a company of mad statesmen.

The Czech state originated in a huge lie and the name of the liar is Beneš.

---

[15] *The New York Times,* September 27, 1938. *The Times* reported further: "Herr Hitler's voice rose to a harsh scream as he pronounced the name of the Czech President. The heils from the audience reached a frantic pitch."

THE BRITISH GUARANTEE TO POLAND, AUGUST 25, 1939[16]

After the Munich Agreement, Hitler proclaimed a protectorate over Bohemia-Moravia, in violation of his solemn promise to guarantee what remained of Czechoslovakia. Britain now gave a guarantee to Poland in a reciprocal treaty of mutual assistance.

✓   ✓   ✓

ARTICLE 1. Should one of the Contracting Parties become engaged in hostilities with a European Power in consequence of aggression by the latter against that Contracting Party, the other Contracting Party will at once give the Contracting Party engaged in hostilities all the support and assistance in its power. . . .

---

[16] *British Command Paper,* No. 6106, p. 37.

CHURCHILL'S THREE FAMOUS SPEECHES OF 1940

The appearance of an extraordinary war leader in times of crisis is traditional in British history. In 1940, when England stood virtually alone against the might of Nazi Germany, Winston Churchill rallied his people with three speeches that have become classics of war literature. The significant sentences follow:

✓   ✓   ✓

Speech of May 13, 1940: "I would say to the House, as I have to those who have joined this Government; 'I have nothing to offer but blood, toil, tears and sweat.' " [17]

Speech of June 18, 1940: "Let us, therefore, brace ourselves to our duty and so bear ourselves that if the British Commonwealth and Empire lasts for a thousand years men will still say, 'This was their finest hour.' " [18]

Speech of August 20, 1940: "Never in the field of human conflict was so much owed by so many to so few" [*British fighter pilots in the Battle of Britain*].[19]

---

[17] *Parliamentary Debates, House of Commons,* 5th series, Vol. CCCLX, p. 1502.
[18] *Ibid.,* Vol. CCCLXII, p. 61.
[19] *Ibid.,* Vol. CCCLXIV, p. 1166.

— Document No. 18 —

PRESIDENT ROOSEVELT'S "FOUR FREEDOMS," JANUARY 6, 1941 [20]

In his address to Congress on January 6, 1941, and reaffirmed in his address of January 6, 1942, President Franklin D. Roosevelt presented his famous "Four Freedoms":

✓ ✓ ✓

. . . In the future days, which we seek to make secure, we look forward to a world founded on four essential human freedoms.

The first is freedom of speech and expression everywhere in the world.

The second is freedom of every person to worship God in his own way everywhere in the world.

The third is freedom from want, which, translated into world terms, means economic understandings which will secure to every nation a healthy peacetime life for its inhabitants everywhere in the world.

The fourth is freedom from fear—which, translated into world terms, means a world-wide reduction of armaments to such a point and in such a thorough fashion that no nation will be in a position to commit an act of physical aggression against any neighbor—anywhere in the world.

[20] *Congressional Record,* LXXXVII (January 6, 1941), p. 46.

·—— Document No. 19 ——

EIGHTH CLAUSE OF THE ATLAN-TIC CHARTER, AUGUST 14, 1941 [21]

On August 14, 1941, President Roosevelt and Prime Minister Churchill issued a joint declaration making known certain common principles in the national policies of their respective countries. This statement of war aims became one of the most famous documents of World War II. The eighth clause concerned disarmament.

Eighth, they believe that all of nations of the world, for realistic as well as spiritual reasons, must come to the abandonment of force. Since no future peace can be maintained if land, sea, or air armaments continue to be employed by nations which threaten, or may threaten aggression outside of their frontiers, they believe, pending the establishment of a wider and permanent system of general security, that the disarmament of such nations is essential. They will likewise aid and encourage all other practicable measures which will lighten for peace-loving peoples the crushing burden of armaments.

(Signed)   Franklin D. Roosevelt
Winston S. Churchill

[21] *Message of President Roosevelt to the Congress, August 21, 1941,* House Document No. 358 (77th Congress, 1st Session) [Washington, 1941].

174

— Document No. 20 —

LEND-LEASE AGREEMENT OF THE UNITED STATES AND GREAT BRITAIN, FEBRUARY 23, 1942[22]

The first Lend-Lease Act was approved by President Roosevelt on March 11, 1941. The Master Mutual Lend-Lease Agreement, signed on February 23, 1942, transformed the United States into an arsenal of democracy. Following are the opening two articles.

✓ ✓ ✓

ARTICLE 1. The Government of the United States of America will continue to supply the Government of the United Kingdom with such defense articles, defense services, and defense information as the President shall authorize to be transferred or provided.

ARTICLE 2. The Government of the United Kingdom will continue to contribute to the defense of the United States of America and the strengthening thereof and will provide such articles, services, facilities or information as it may be in a position to supply.

[22] Department of State Publication 1790, *United States Executive Agreement Series,* No. 241 (Washington, 1942).

175

— Document No. 21 —

ORIGIN OF THE TERM, "UNCONDITIONAL SURRENDER," JANUARY 24, 1943 [23]

In January, 1943, after the Allied landings in North Africa, Roosevelt and Churchill met at Casablanca in French Morocco. Surveying the entire field of the war theatre by theatre, they agreed that all resources were to be marshalled for the more intense prosecution of the war by sea, land, and air. At the close of the conference, Roosevelt and Churchill, together with Generals de Gaulle and Giraud, convened on the lawn of the villa to meet thirty foreign correspondents. The official communiqué of the conference had not mentioned the words "unconditional surrender," which were used by Roosevelt in the press interview. This was the first reference to the official Allied objective of the war—a phrase that ruled out any negotiations with Germany through the channels of diplomatic negotiation. Critics later claimed that another less harsh phrase, such as "honorable capitulation," might have encouraged the Germans to surrender long before they did.

✓   ✓   ✓

Another point I think we have all had it in our hearts and heads before, but I don't think it has ever been put down on paper by the Prime Minister and myself, and that is the determination that peace can come to the world only by the total elimination of German and Japanese war power.

[23] 875th Press Conference, Joint Conference by President Roosevelt and Prime Minister Churchill at Casablanca, January 24, 1943. *The Public Papers and Addresses of Franklin D. Roosevelt*, compiled by Samuel I. Rosenman (New York, 1943), Vol. X, p. 39.

Some of you Britishers know the old story—we had a General called U. S. Grant. His name was Ulysses Simpson Grant, but in my, and the Prime Minister's, early days he was called "Unconditional Surrender" Grant. The elimination of German, Japanese, and Italian war power means the unconditional surrender by Germany, Italy, and Japan. That means a reasonable assurance of future world peace. It does not mean the destruction of the population of Germany, Italy, or Japan, but it does mean the destruction of the philosophies in those countries which are based on conquest and the subjugation of other people.

— Document No. 22 —

DISPUTED CLAUSES OF THE SECRET TREATY OF YALTA, FEBRUARY 11, 1945 [24]

In February, 1945, Roosevelt, Churchill, and Stalin concluded a secret agreement, the terms of which were not revealed for a year, providing that Russia would enter the war against Japan in return for certain territorial guarantees after victory. After the war, critics of Roosevelt denounced him for what they called unwarranted concessions; defenders insisted that no one knew at the time how long it would take to subjugate Japan. The disputed clauses of the treaty follow.

[24] Text in Robert Ergang, *Europe in Our Time* (Boston, 1953), p. 618.

2. The former rights of Russia violated by the treacherous attack of Japan shall be restored, viz.:

a. The southern part of Sakhalin as well as the islands adjacent to it shall be returned to the Soviet Union;

b. The commercial port of Dairen shall be internationalized, the preëminent interests of the Soviet Union in this port being safeguarded, and the lease of Port Arthur as a naval base of U.S.S.R. restored;

c. The Chinese Eastern Railroad and the South Manchurian Railroad, which provides an outlet to Dairen, shall be jointly operated by the establishment of a joint Soviet-Chinese company, it being understood that the preëminent interests of the Soviet Union shall be safeguarded and that China shall retain full sovereignty in Manchuria;

3. The Kurile Islands shall be handed over to the Soviet Union. . . .

Joseph V. Stalin
Franklin D. Roosevelt
Winston C. Churchill

— Document No. 23 —

ORIGIN OF THE POINT-FOUR PROGRAM, JANUARY 20, 1949 [25]

In his inaugural address of January 20, 1949, President Harry S. Truman announced four major courses of action by the United States for peace and freedom. The

[25] *Inaugural Address of Harry S. Truman,* Senate Document No. 4 (81st Congress, 1st Session) [Washington, 1949], pp. 3-4.

first pledged unfaltering support to the United Nations; the second called for a continuation of a program for world economic recovery; and the third promised the strengthening of freedom-loving nations against dangers of aggression. The famous Point IV follows.

✓   ✓   ✓

Fourth. We must embark on a bold new program for making the benefit of our scientific advances and industrial progress available for the improvement and growth of underdeveloped areas.

More than half the people of the world are living in conditions approaching misery. Their food is inadequate. They are victims of disease. Their economic life is primitive and stagnant. Their poverty is a handicap and a threat both to them and to more prosperous areas.

For the first time in history, humanity possesses the knowledge and the skill to relieve the suffering of these people.

The United States is preëminent among nations in the development of industrial and scientific techniques. The material resources which we can afford to use for the assistance of other peoples are limited. But our imponderable resources in technical knowledge are constantly growing and are inexhaustible.

I believe that we should make available to peace-loving peoples the benefits of our store of technical knowledge in order to help them realize their aspirations for a better life. And, in coöperation with other nations, we should foster capital development in areas needing development.

Our aim should be to help the free peoples of the world, through their own efforts, to produce more food, more clothing, more materials for housing, and more mechanical power to lighten their burdens. . . .

Only by helping the least fortunate of its members to help themselves can the human family achieve the decent, satisfying life that is the right of all people.

Democracy alone can supply the vitalizing force to stir the peoples of the world into triumphant action, not only against their human oppressors, but also against their ancient enemies—hunger, misery, and despair. . . .

ARTICLE 5 OF THE NORTH ATLANTIC TREATY, APRIL 4, 1949 [26]

On April 4, 1949, twelve states (Belgium, Canada, Denmark, France, Iceland, Italy, Luxemburg, the Netherlands, Norway, Portugal, the United Kingdom, and the United States) [27] signed a treaty in Washington calling for the integrated defense of the North Atlantic area. The *casus belli* was expressed in Article 5, the essence of the treaty.

ARTICLE 5. The Parties agree that an armed attack against one or more of them in Europe or North America shall be considered an attack against them all; and consequently they agree that, if such an armed attack occurs, each of them, in exercise of the right of individual or collective self-defense recognized by Article 51 of the Charter of the United Nations, will assist the Party or Parties so attacked by taking forthwith, individually and in concert with the other Parties, such action as it deems necessary, including the use of armed force, to restore and maintain the security of the North Atlantic area.

Any such armed attack and all measures taken as a result thereof shall immediately be reported to the Security Council. Such measures shall be terminated when the Security Council has taken the measures necessary to restore and maintain international peace and security.

[26] *North Atlantic Treaty,* Document No. 48 in *Documents Relating to the North Atlantic Treaty* (81st Congress 1st Session) [Washington, 1949], p. 2.

[27] The membership of NATO was extended later to 14 by the addition of Greece and Turkey (1952).

— Document No. 25 —

THE TEST BAN TREATY, 1963 [28]

An opportunity to reduce world tensions came on July 25, 1963, when the United States, the United Kingdom, and the Soviet Union signed at Moscow a treaty banning nuclear weapon tests in the atmosphere, in outer space, and under water. This treaty was designed to free the world from fear of radioactive fallout and to prevent the spread of nuclear weapons. Following is the text of the treaty.

✶   ✶   ✶

The Governments of the United States of America, the United Kingdom of Great Britain and Northern Ireland, and the Union of Soviet Socialist Republics, hereinafter referred to as the "Original Parties",

Proclaiming as their principal aim the speediest possible achievement of an agreement on general and complete disarmament under strict international control in accordance with the objectives of the United Nations which would put an end to the armaments race and eliminate the incentive to the production and testing of all kinds of weapons, including nuclear weapons,

Seeking to achieve the discontinuance of all test explosions of nuclear weapons for all time, determined to continue negotiations to this end, and desiring to put an end to the contamination of man's environment by radioactive substances,

Have agreed as follows:

Article I

1. Each of the Parties to this Treaty undertakes to prohibit, to prevent, and not to carry out any nuclear

[28] *U.S. Department of State Bulletin,* Vol. XLIX, August 12, 1963, pp. 239-240.

weapon test explosion, or any other nuclear explosion, at any place under its jurisdiction or control:

(a) in the atmosphere; beyond its limits, including outer space; or underwater, including territorial waters or high seas; or

(b) in any other environment if such explosion causes radioactive debris to be present outside the territorial limits of the State under whose jurisdiction or control such explosion is conducted. It is understood in this connection that the provisions of this subparagraph are without prejudice to the conclusion of a treaty resulting in the permanent banning of all nuclear test explosions, including all such explosions underground, the conclusion of which, as the Parties have stated in the Preamble to this Treaty, they seek to achieve.

2. Each of the Parties to this Treaty undertakes furthermore to refrain from causing, encouraging, or in any way participating in, the carrying out of any nuclear weapon test explosion, or any other nuclear explosion, anywhere which would take place in any of the environments described, or have the effect referred to, in paragraph 1 of this Article.

Article II

1. Any Party may propose amendments to this Treaty. The text of any proposed amendment shall be submitted to the Depositary Governments which shall circulate it to all Parties to this Treaty. Thereafter, if requested to do so by one-third or more of the Parties, the Depositary Governments shall convene a conference, to which they shall invite all the Parties, to consider such amendment.

2. Any amendment to this Treaty must be approved by a majority of the votes of all the Parties to this Treaty, including the votes of all of the Original Parties. The amendment shall enter into force for all Parties upon the deposit of instruments of ratification by a majority of all of the Original Parties.

Article III

1. This Treaty shall be open to all States for signature. Any State which does not sign this Treaty before its

entry into force in accordance with paragraph 3 of this Article may accede to it at any time.

2. This Treaty shall be subject to ratification by signatory States. Instruments of ratification and instruments of accession shall be deposited with the Governments of the Original Parties—the United States of America, the United Kingdom of Great Britain and Northern Ireland, and the Union of Soviet Socialist Republics—which are hereby designated the Depositary Governments.

3. This Treaty shall enter into force after its ratification by all the Original Parties and the deposit of their instruments of ratification.

4. For States whose instruments of ratification or accession are deposited subsequent to the entry into force of this Treaty, it shall enter into force on the date of the deposit of their instruments of ratification or accession.

5. The Depositary Governments shall promptly inform all signatory and acceding States of the date of each signature, the date of deposit of each instrument of ratification of and accession to this Treaty, the date of its entry into force, and the date of receipt of any requests for conferences or other notices.

6. This Treaty shall be registered by the Depositary Governments pursuant to Article 102 of the Charter of the United Nations.

Article IV

This Treaty shall be of unlimited duration.

Each Party shall in exercising its national sovereignty have the right to withdraw from the Treaty if it decides that extraordinary events, related to the subject matter of this Treaty, have jeopardized the supreme interests of its country. It shall give notice of such withdrawal to all other Parties to the Treaty three months in advance.

Article V

This Treaty, of which the English and Russian texts are equally authentic, shall be deposited in the archives of the Depositary Governments. Duly certified copies of this Treaty shall be transmitted by the Depositary Governments to the Governments of the signatory and acceding States.

RECOMMENDED READING

Albjerg, Victor L., and Marguerite Albjerg, *From Sedan to Stresa: Europe Since 1870* (New York, 1937).

Baltzly, Alexander, and A. William Salomone, *Readings in Twentieth-Century European History* (New York, 1950).

Benns, F. L., *Europe Since 1914 in its World Setting* (New York, 1945).

Black, C. E., and E. C. Helmreich, *Twentieth Century Europe* (New York, 1959).

Bruun, Geoffrey, *The World in the Twentieth Century* (Boston, 1952).

Chambers, Frank P., Christina Phelps Harris, and Charles C. Bayley, *This Age of Conflict: A Contemporary World History* (New York, 1950).

Commager, Henry Steele, *Documents of World History* (New York, 1942).

Cooke, W. H., and E. P. Stickney, *Readings in European International Relations Since 1871* (New York, 1939).

Ergang, Robert R., *Europe in Our Time* (Boston, 1958).

Hall, Walter Phelps, *Europe in the Twentieth Century* (New York, 1957).

Halphen, L., and P. Sagnac, eds., *Peuples et civilisations* (Paris, 1926 ff).

Hawgood, J. E., *Modern Constitutions* (New York, 1938).

Hayes, Carlton J. H., *Nationalism: A Religion* (New York, 1960).

Holborn, Hajo, *The Political Collapse of Europe* (New York, 1951).

Hughes, H. Stuart, *Contemporary Europe: A History* (Englewood Cliffs, N.J., 1961).

Kedourie, Elie, *Nationalism* (New York, 1960).

Kohn, Hans, *The Twentieth Century: Midway Account of the Western World* (New York, 1949).

Kohn, Hans, *The Age of Nationalism* (New York, 1962).

Langsam, Walter C., *The World Since 1870* (New York, 1963).

Langsam, Walter C., and J. M. Eagen, eds., *Documents and Readings in the History of Europe since 1918* (New York, 1951).

May, Arthur James, *Europe and Two World Wars* (New York, 1947).

Mumford, Lewis, *Technics and Civilization* (New York, 1934).

Schapiro, J. Salwyn, *The World in Crisis* (New York, 1950).

Setton, Kenneth M., and Henry R. Winkler, *Great Problems in European Civilization* (Englewood Cliffs, N.J., 1962).

Snyder, Louis L., *The Imperialism Reader* (Princeton, 1962).

Snyder, Louis L., *The Dynamics of Nationalism* (Princeton, 1964).

Swain, Joseph W., *Beginning the Twentieth Century* (New York, 1938).

Toynbee, Arnold J., and others, *Survey of International Affairs* (Oxford, 1921-1938).

Vermeil, Edmond, *1914-1950,* in Barker, Sir Ernest, and others, *The European Inheritance* (Oxford, 1954), Vol. III, pp. 187-292.

Wheeler-Bennett, J. W., *Documents on International Affairs* (Oxford, 1928-40).

Wright, Gordon, and Arthur Mejia, Jr., *An Age of Controversy* (New York, 1963).

— APPENDIX —

USE OF THE VETO
IN THE UNITED NATIONS *

List of instances in which proposals before the Security Council obtained the required 7 affirmative votes out of 11 (5 permanent and 6 non-permanent members) but were not carried as a result of the negative vote of one or more *permanent* members of the Security Council.

Question Before Security Council	Date	Permanent Member Voting in Negative
1. Syrian and Lebanese question: withdrawal of foreign troops	Feb. 16, 1946	U.S.S.R.
2. Spanish question: investigation of Franco regime	June 18, 1946	U.S.S.R.
3. Spanish question: resolution for observation of	June 26, 1946	U.S.S.R.
4. Spanish question: vote on President's ruling	June 26, 1946	U.S.S.R., France
5. Spanish question: resolution	June 26, 1946	U.S.S.R.
6. Admission: Transjordan	Aug. 29, 1946	U.S.S.R.
7. Admission: Ireland	Aug. 29, 1946	U.S.S.R.
8. Admission: Portugal	Aug. 29, 1946	U.S.S.R.
9. Greek question: border incidents	Sept. 20, 1946	U.S.S.R.
10. Corfu Channel question	Mar. 25, 1947	U.S.S.R.
11. Greek question: U.S. recommendation	July 29, 1947	U.S.S.R.

* For this list I am indebted to several sources: the Department of Public Information, Research Section, United Nations; W. Chamberlain and T. Hovet, Jr., *A Chronology and Fact Book of the United Nations, 1941-1961* (New York, 1961); the *United Nations Review*; the *Yearbook of the United Nations*; and *The New York Times*. There is no official document in the United Nations on the vetoes, nor is there a procedure for keeping it up-to-date. There is a difference of opinion on exact numbers in the list. My count shows 106 vetoes, of which the U.S.S.R. cast 101. *The New York Times* lists the Goa veto (December 18, 1961) as the 99th Soviet veto.

Question Before Security Council	Date	Permanent Member Voting in Negative
12. Admission: Transjordan	Aug. 18, 1947	U.S.S.R.
13. Admission: Ireland	Aug. 18, 1947	U.S.S.R.
14. Admission: Portugal	Aug. 18, 1947	U.S.S.R.
15. Greek question: northern borders	Aug. 19, 1947	U.S.S.R.
16. Greek question: guerrillas	Aug. 19, 1947	U.S.S.R.
17. Admission: Italy	Aug. 21, 1947	U.S.S.R.
18. Admission: Austria	Aug. 21, 1947	U.S.S.R.
19. Indonesian question: cease-fire	Aug. 25, 1947	France
20. Greek question: to Assembly	Sept. 15, 1947	U.S.S.R.
21. Greek question: procedural	Sept. 15, 1947	U.S.S.R.
22. Admission: Italy	Oct. 1, 1947	U.S.S.R.
23. Admission: Finland	Oct. 1, 1947	U.S.S.R.
24. Admission: Italy	Apr. 10, 1948	U.S.S.R.
25. Czechoslovak question: procedural	May 24, 1948	U.S.S.R.
26. Czechoslovak question: situation in	May 24, 1948	U.S.S.R.
27. Atomic Energy Commission: reports	June 22, 1948	U.S.S.R.
28. Admission: Ceylon	Aug. 18, 1948	U.S.S.R.
29. Berlin question: to prevent discord	Oct. 25, 1948	U.S.S.R.
30. Admission: Ceylon	Dec. 15, 1948	U.S.S.R.
31. Admission: Republic of Korea	Apr. 8, 1949	U.S.S.R.
32. Admission: Nepal	Sept. 7, 1949	U.S.S.R.
33. Admission: Portugal	Sept. 13, 1949	U.S.S.R.
34. Admission: Transjordan	Sept. 13, 1949	U.S.S.R.
35. Admission: Italy	Sept. 13, 1949	U.S.S.R.
36. Admission: Finland	Sept. 13, 1949	U.S.S.R.
37. Admission: Ireland	Sept. 13, 1949	U.S.S.R.
38. Admission: Austria	Sept. 13, 1949	U.S.S.R.
39. Admission: Ceylon	Sept. 13, 1949	U.S.S.R.
40. Regulation and reduction of armaments	Oct. 11, 1949	U.S.S.R.
41. Regulation and reduction of armaments: census	Oct. 18, 1949	U.S.S.R.
42. Regulation and reduction of armaments	Oct. 18, 1949	U.S.S.R.
43. Indonesian question: welcome to Republic	Dec. 13, 1949	U.S.S.R.
44. Indonesian question: Canadian resolution on	Dec. 13, 1949	U.S.S.R.
45. Complaint of aggression upon Republic of Korea	Sept. 6, 1950	U.S.S.R.
46. Complaint of bombing of territory of China by air forces	Sept. 12, 1950	U.S.S.R.
47. Appointment of Secretary-General	Oct. 12, 1950	U.S.S.R.
48. Complaint of aggression upon Republic of Korea	Nov. 30, 1950	U.S.S.R.
49. Admission: Italy	Feb. 6, 1952	U.S.S.R.
50. Request for investigation of bacteriological warfare in Korea	July 3, 1952	U.S.S.R.

Question Before Security Council	Date	Permanent Member Voting in Negative
51. Request for investigation of bacteriological warfare	July 9, 1952	U.S.S.R.
52. Admission: Libya	Sept. 16, 1952	U.S.S.R.
53. Admission: Japan	Sept. 18, 1952	U.S.S.R.
54. Admission: Vietnam	Sept. 19, 1952	U.S.S.R.
55. Admission: Laos	Sept. 19, 1952	U.S.S.R.
56. Admission: Cambodia	Sept. 19, 1952	U.S.S.R.
57. Appointment of Secretary-General	Mar. 13, 1953	1 negative vote by permanent member; not identified; meeting held in private (Chamberlain and Hovet identify as U.S.S.R.)
58. Palestine question: peace between Israel and Syria	Jan. 22, 1954	U.S.S.R.
59. Palestine question: Suez	Mar. 29, 1954	U.S.S.R.
60. Request of Thailand for observers	June 18, 1954	U.S.S.R.
61. Complaint of Guatemala	June 20, 1954	U.S.S.R.
62. Admission: Republic of Korea	Dec. 13, 1955	U.S.S.R.
63. Admission: Vietnam	Dec. 13, 1955	U.S.S.R.
64. Admission: Mongolian People's Republic	Dec. 13, 1955	China
65. Admission: Jordan	Dec. 13, 1955	U.S.S.R.
66. Admission: Ireland	Dec. 13, 1955	U.S.S.R.
67. Admission: Portugal	Dec. 13, 1955	U.S.S.R.
68. Admission: Italy	Dec. 13, 1955	U.S.S.R.
69. Admission: Austria	Dec. 13, 1955	U.S.S.R.
70. Admission: Finland	Dec. 13, 1955	U.S.S.R.
71. Admission: Ceylon	Dec. 13, 1955	U.S.S.R.
72. Admission: Ceylon	Dec. 13, 1955	U.S.S.R.
73. Admission: Libya	Dec. 13, 1955	U.S.S.R.
74. Admission: Cambodia	Dec. 13, 1955	U.S.S.R.
75. Admission: Japan	Dec. 13, 1955	U.S.S.R.
76. Admission: Laos	Dec. 13, 1955	U.S.S.R.
77. Admission: Spain	Dec. 13, 1955	U.S.S.R.
78. Admission: Japan	Dec. 14, 1955	U.S.S.R.
79. Admission: Japan	Dec. 15, 1955	U.S.S.R.
80. Suez Canal question	Oct. 13, 1956	U.S.S.R.
81. Palestine question: France and United Kingdom to refrain in	Oct. 30, 1956	France United Kingdom
82. Palestine question: Israel to refrain in	Oct. 30, 1956	France United Kingdom
83. Situation in Hungary: U.S.S.R. to desist in	Nov. 4, 1956	U.S.S.R.
84. India-Pakistan question: possible U.N. force in Kashmir	Feb. 20, 1957	U.S.S.R.
85. Admission: Republic of Korea	Sept. 9, 1957	U.S.S.R.
86. Admission: Vietnam	Sept. 9, 1957	U.S.S.R.
87. U.S.S.R. complaint on U.S. flights in Arctic	May 2, 1958	U.S.S.R.

Question Before Security Council	Date	Permanent Member Voting in Negative
88. Lebanon: U.S. proposal for measures in	July 18, 1958	U.S.S.R.
89. Lebanon: Japanese proposal on U.S. withdrawal from	July 22, 1958	U.S.S.R.
90. Admission: Republic of Korea	Dec. 9, 1958	U.S.S.R.
91. Admission: Vietnam	Dec. 9, 1958	U.S.S.R.
92. U.S.S.R. complaint regarding violation of frontiers by U.S. Air Force	July 26, 1960	U.S.S.R.
93. U.S.S.R. complaint on violation of frontiers by U.S. Air Force	July 26, 1960	U.S.S.R.
94. Situation in Congo: Ceylon-Tunesian proposal on	Sept. 17, 1960	U.S.S.R.
95. Admission: Islamic Republic of Mauretania	Dec. 3, 1960	U.S.S.R.
96. Congo: law and order in	Dec. 13, 1960	U.S.S.R.
97. Congo: situation in	Feb. 20, 1961	U.S.S.R.
98. Congo: situation in	Feb. 20, 1961	U.S.S.R.
99. Kuwait: British resolution on	July 7, 1961	U.S.S.R.
100. Congo: situation in	Nov. 24, 1961	U.S.S.R.
101. Congo: situation in	Nov. 24, 1961	U.S.S.R.
102. Admission: Kuwait	Nov. 30, 1961	U.S.S.R.
103. Complaint by Portugal on situation in Goa, Damao, and Diu	Dec. 18, 1961	U.S.S.R.
104. India-Pakistan question: appeal for negotiations	June 22, 1962	U.S.S.R.
105. Palestine: condemning murder of two Israeli citizens	Sept. 3, 1963	U.S.S.R.
106. Southern Rhodesia: calling on United Kingdom to halt proposed transfer of governmental powers and armed forces to Southern Rhodesia	Sept. 13, 1963	United Kingdom

INDEX